E. Kent 08.

D0714525

THE SUSPECT

Jenny Friel

THE SUSPECT

The Story of Rachel O'Reilly's Murder

Every effort has been made to contact the copyright holders of material reproduced in this text. In cases where these efforts have been unsuccessful, the copyright holders are asked to contact the publishers directly.

First published in 2007 by Maverick House Publishers.
Maverick House, Office 19, Dunboyne Business Park, Dunboyne, Co. Meath, Ireland.
Maverick House Asia, Level 41, United Centre, 323 Silom Road, Bangrak, Bangkok 10500, Thailand.

info@maverickhouse.com
http://www.maverickhouse.com

ISBN: 978 1 905379 41 5

Copyright for text © 2007 Jenny Friel.
Copyright for typesetting, editing, layout, design © Maverick Publishing Ltd.

5 4 3 2 1

The paper used in this book comes from wood pulp of managed forests. For every tree felled, at least one tree is planted, thereby renewing natural resources.

The moral rights of the author have been asserted.

All rights reserved.
No part of this book may be reproduced or transmitted in any form or by any means without written permission from the publisher, except by a reviewer who wishes to quote brief passages in connection with a review written for insertion in a newspaper, magazine or broadcast.

A CIP catalogue record for this book is available from the British Library.

ACKNOWLEDGEMENTS

I'D LIKE TO thank my bosses at the *Irish Mail on Sunday*, Paul Drury and Ted Verity, for allowing me the time to complete this project and for their encouragement.

Special thanks to my colleagues Valerie Hanley, Mary Carr and Patrice Harrington for their unfailing interest and support. Also huge thanks to Chris Bacon, Tom Honan and Michael Chester for their images and to James Meehan for his help with pictures. Many thanks to Shane Phelan, Kathy Sheridan and Darren Boyle for their generosity with their time and their work.

I greatly appreciate Dr Robi Ludwig making the effort to talk with me and share her expertise.

Thanks also to the team at Maverick House Publishers.

A huge thank you to so many of my friends for their support and enthusiasm. Special thanks to Karen Rice for her invaluable advice, to Lindsay Campbell for her generous assistance to David (Jasper) Gallagher for his help in sourcing research material. And to Kerry-Anne McCarthy and her dad Kerry for copy-proofing and suggestions.

I am very grateful to my family for their infinite patience and understanding, and a huge big thank you to Mark Gallagher for his constant support and serenity.

INTRODUCTION

WITH THE SOUND of her heart pounding loudly in her ears, Rose Callaly drove as quickly as she could in the direction of her daughter's home.

Gripping the steering wheel tightly, she did her best to calm herself down by going through all of the logical reasons why Rachel O'Reilly might not be answering her telephone.

Maybe she was out shopping or visiting a friend and had left her mobile at home by mistake, maybe there was a fault with the line, maybe … Rose shook her head and decided to concentrate on the road instead; it was safer that way.

Thankfully traffic was good and within 20 minutes she was parking in the driveway of her daughter's bungalow, which lay nestled in the picturesque countryside of north Dublin.

As she pulled up beside Rachel's Renault Scenic, which was parked in the same spot she always left it, Rose's sense of foreboding deepened. If her daughter was at home, why had she not answered the landline or acknowledged any of the many worried messages her family had left for her?

Ever since being told that her daughter had failed to pick up her youngest son, Adam, from the crèche

7

earlier that morning, Rose knew from somewhere deep down that something was wrong.

But now was not the time to panic; she had to find Rachel.

As she turned off the engine of her car, two dogs her daughter was looking after began to jump and bark. Already in a rush to get into the house, she was irritated by the thoughts of trying to stop them following her.

As it was, she needn't have worried—something was already stopping the dogs from entering the house.

Walking quickly to the back patio doors of the house, the entrance the family always used, Rose was surprised to find them both wide open. She was even more surprised when she saw that the curtains in the kitchen were drawn, something Rachel would never allow happen during the day.

She entered and swiftly scanned the room and although paying little attention, as she was intent on locating Rachel, she did notice there were several items strewn around the floor.

She would later recall that she felt 'someone had taken and actually placed them there.' She also spotted that the kitchen tap was running but did not stop to turn it off.

'Rachel, Rachel, where are you love?' Rose called as she walked into the utility room. There was no sign of her daughter in the small area where the washing machine was kept, so she crossed over into the hallway. Turning to her left, she checked the sitting room; it was a mess, dozens of CDs and DVDs lay strewn on the floor. What had happened? Where was Rachel?

Rose began to call louder.

'Rachel, Rachel are you alright? Answer me love. Where are you?'

Hurrying down the narrow corridor towards the bedrooms, the anxiousness she had been feeling was slowly turning into something more sinister, it was now closer to terror.

Over and over again she called her daughter's name, and reaching the end of the hallway she looked first into the bedroom on the right that her two grandsons, Luke and Adam, shared. Everything appeared to be normal and so she turned around to face the room where her daughter slept with her husband Joe.

Her eyes were almost immediately and reluctantly drawn to the floor.

Blessing herself, she let out a small cry. There, lying motionless on the light coloured carpet of the room was the body of her daughter, Rachel.

Her hair, which was obscuring her face, was matted with something thick, sticky and dark. It took Rose several moments to realise it was blood. She forced herself to look closer, it was clear that Rachel had suffered some kind of horrific injury to her head. In fact, the wounds to her skull had bled so badly that Rose could not even tell if her daughter's face was lying sideways or straight down on the carpet.

There was a large pool of blood under her head; it was thick and congealed and as Rose knelt there, beside her daughter's body, she found herself thinking it was the very same colour as beetroot.

As she scanned Rachel's body for any signs of life, she noticed her torso was twisted as though she had fallen awkwardly. Her left arm was out-stretched, almost like she was reaching for something.

Rose fell to her knees. 'Rachel, Rachel, what's happened to you? Come on Rachel, talk to me, please, wake-up. Rachel, you'll be fine, I'll get help.'

As she pleaded with her daughter to open her eyes, Rose rubbed Rachel's arms, in the vain hope that it might help wake her. Rachel's skin was like marble.

Distraught, almost bordering on hysterical, Rose bent over the lifeless body and continued talking to Rachel, reassuring her daughter that everything was going to be OK and that help was on its way. But Rose knew it was already too late.

'As soon as I saw her I knew she was dead and I knew she was murdered,' she said later, '…and I knew she was dead a while. I just kept talking to her.'

The murder of Rachel O'Reilly—a popular, vivacious, 30-year-old mother of two—prompted one of the most high profile garda investigations Ireland has ever seen.

At first the horrific crime was believed to have been the work of a startled burglar, but soon the spotlight had fallen firmly on the victim's husband, Joe, a 32-year-old advertising executive.

Although he worked hard at playing the part of a grieving widower, begging the public for their assistance to catch his beloved wife's killer; it became clear that all was not what it seemed with the 6ft 5in Dubliner.

Family and friends of Rachel's later told how they first began to notice his odd behaviour at her funeral, where he made several of them uncomfortable with the strange nature of his macabre conversations.

The public first became aware of bad feeling between Joe and Rachel's family, the Callalys, during an appearance on *The Late Late Show* three weeks after Rachel's death when it was claimed that Rose was openly cold towards her son-in-law. And some viewers believed Joe seemed to be taking his wife's death much too easily in his stride.

It was then revealed that Joe, contrary to the impression he had given in several newspaper interviews, had been far from a devoted husband. In fact, he had been cheating on Rachel for some time with former work colleague, Nikki Pelley.

The media, already gripped by the investigation of the shocking and brutal murder of an ordinary housewife in the bedroom of her own home, were now utterly enthralled.

In fact, it proved to be one of the most intense, publicised and most talked about murder cases since the murder of Tom Nevin by his wife Catherine, whom the tabloids nicknamed The Black Widow.

Over the next two years hardly a month went by without a story about Rachel's murder and her husband Joe, a self-professed suspect in the case, appearing on the front page of some national newspaper.

Joe's face became instantly recognisable, as did his wife's. The circulation of some newspapers were said to have increased by several thousand every time they published a picture of Rachel on their front covers.

But regardless of the numerous reports of how gardaí were 'close to a break through', and officers were confident of 'charging a man with the murder within days', it seemed, at times, as though the case might never be solved.

In November 2006, however, it was deemed there was enough evidence to charge Joe with the murder and send him to stand trial before a jury of his peers. The court date was set for June 2007. All anyone could do was wait.

Much of what follows was taken from evidence presented to the Central Criminal Court during the trial of Joe O'Reilly, which resulted in his conviction for the murder of his wife, Rachel.

The summer of 2007 will be remembered for two things—the atrocious weather and the trial of Joe O'Reilly.

It appeared that everyone in Ireland had an opinion; taxi drivers spoke of little else and in every pub around the country, conversation was dominated by the facts of the case and whether or not Joe would be found guilty.

From the day the hearing began on 27 June, almost every word uttered by every witness and every piece of evidence produced was reported by the scores of journalists sent to cover the case from start to finish. And every day hoards of curious on-lookers arrived at the court, determined to catch a glimpse of Joe, scrutinising his face for any expression of guilt or remorse, analysing his body language to try to get a better idea of the man whose face had become so familiar to them over the previous couple of years.

It was to be one of the most emotional and dramatic trials ever witnessed in Ireland, largely due to the nature of the evidence that seemed to be revealed on a daily basis.

Seasoned court reporters told how it was like nothing they had every experienced before and spoke in astonishment of the barrage of disturbing testimony that was making it onto the front pages of most newspapers almost every day for a month.

And then there was the Callaly family. The sight of Rose, her husband Jimmy and their four remaining children, Declan, Paul, Anne and Anthony arriving at the courts complex each morning, predominantly dressed in black, made an extraordinarily powerful image and one that the public is unlikely to ever forget.

United in their grief and their blatant lust for justice for Rachel, they sat in the same positions on the same bench for 21 days, listening intently to every piece of business that went before the court.

Although impressively strong and brave throughout some horrendous evidence about the murder of their Rachel, they were clear from the beginning who they believed was responsible for her death.

And then there was Joe's family, the O'Reillys.

At first, he was accompanied by just his mother Ann, who arrived at court at the same time every day to sit on the very last bench of the courtroom.

For three weeks it was just the two of them, arriving together, going for lunch together, and going home together at the end of another exhausting day.

During the last week, they were joined by Joe's older brother Derek, and on the very last day, the day of the verdict, his sister Ann was also present, to hold her mother's hand as the jury told the courtroom of their decision.

But it was not only the families or those directly involved who fervently waited for a conclusion to this remarkable trial.

People told later of how they were on holiday on the continent when the verdict was finally delivered. And how cheers rang out through apartment blocks and poolside areas as the word of the result quickly spread.

Others related how wedding receptions around Ireland were interrupted to share the news that the Joe O'Reilly trial was finally over.

It is hard to pinpoint exactly why the murder trial attracted almost an insatiable level of interest for so long—but there are many theories.

First of all the murder of an innocent young mum, killed in the relative safety of her own bedroom after dropping her children off to school, without any apparent motive, is always something that will capture our attention as it sends an involuntary shiver down our spines.

There was also the brutal nature of the murder itself—the victim was battered to death over the head with a 'heavy blunt instrument'. It was almost too gruesome to comprehend.

And when rumours began to circulate of the possible involvement of her husband, the public's interest was piqued even further because Joe and Rachel appeared to the outside world to be a perfectly, if not enviably, happy young couple, with two gorgeous boys, a house they had dreamed of, a battalion of loyal friends and loving families on both sides to help and support them.

And maybe it was because Joe was described by most people who actually knew him or met him as a pretty unremarkable kind of guy, friendly and articulate.

I met him several times over ten months or so, and thought him to be a nice man, the kind of person who liked to be liked.

Friends and those who socialized with him believed him to be unfailingly kind, considerate, if not sweet, and though they may have been aware the couple had experienced problems, well, what couple doesn't?

But probably the most enthralling thing about the O'Reillys was that they were ordinary and utterly normal. They lived in an ordinary, close-knit area that had never experienced something of this nature before.

They held down ordinary jobs and, although by no means wealthy, they were financially stable and were able to afford the kind of luxuries a lot of us take for granted these days; two cars, the odd foreign holiday as well as savings for a decent education for their children.

In fact, this was a couple that could have lived beside any of us, who could have been our friends, or who could have been our brother, our sister, our son or our daughter.

It was their apparent ordinariness that set them apart and is what made Joe's inexplicable and heinous crime all the more difficult to fathom.

Why didn't he just take care of his problem, the fact that he obviously no longer wanted to be married to Rachel, in the same way most, if not all, of us would have? Why did he not file for divorce or separate?

Why did he meticulously plan and then carry out the brutal killing of the mother of his two little boys?

We will probably never know for sure. All we do know is that Joe thought he had gotten away with it; he thought he had been clever and devious enough to carry out the perfect murder.

Even he must now see the irony in his own words: 'I've no doubt that whoever did this will be caught. They've already proved they're not that clever or brave so they're bound to slip up.'

CHAPTER 1

Growing Up and Young Love

JOE O'REILLY grew up in Kilbarrack, a working class suburb of North Dublin.

His parents, Joseph O'Reilly Senior and Ann (nee Lynch), had moved to the area from Drimnagh in the south of the city. The couple had married in the late 1960s, a couple of years after first meeting in a dancehall on Camden Street.

In the beginning things were good. Joe Senior worked for the Dublin Corporation while Ann was kept busy at home, taking care of their children. First there was Derek, followed by Joe who was born on 6 April 1972, and then their sister Ann Jnr.

But then their youngest daughter Martina was born. It must have been heartbreaking for the couple to learn that their baby daughter was born blind with Down's Syndrome. But Ann O'Reilly was determined Martina should get the best care possible and worked hard to ensure she was always taken care of.

Another enormous upset for the family occurred in 1976 when Joe was four years old.

His uncle and Ann's brother, Christy Lynch, was convicted of murder, but this conviction was quashed, and he was declared an innocent man, having spent years in prison.

It was a landmark case that set a precedent in the Irish justice system. It also affected the O'Reilly's view of the legal system, perhaps understandably.

As a teenager Joe and his siblings attended the Greendale Community School. Even though he was the second eldest, he was the natural leader among the O'Reilly children. It helped that he also had a physically commanding presence from a young age, towering over the rest of his family from his mid-teens. But while the rest of his childhood years passed smoothly, during his late teens Joe's parents' relationship began to disintegrate.

His father, Joe Snr, left for England, where he still lives today.

'It came to a stage where it was all too much for me,' Joe O'Reilly Senior would later tell a reporter. [1]

'Joseph was studying for important exams, so when the marriage broke up I decided to leave Ireland altogether.'

While Joe maintained contact with his father over the phone, the only time he went to visit him in Britain was several years later, when he brought his then girlfriend, Rachel, over to introduce her to her future father-in-law.

It is hard to fathom the kind of impact his father's absence might have had on a young Joe. But perhaps it is one of the reasons he was so determined to remain a full-time figure in his own children's lives—no matter what it took.

*****

Less than a couple of miles away from where Joe was growing up, Rachel Callaly was busy making friends and thinking up new ways to use up her remarkable stores of energy.

Rachel began life on 10 October 1973, as Theresa Green, where she was born to a seventeen-year-old Dublin girl of the same name.

Her mother immediately decided to give her little baby up for adoption. Given her young age and the conservatism of Ireland in the early 1970s, it was an understandable choice.

Luckily for Jim and Rose Callaly, it meant they now had a little girl to join their family. The couple had already adopted two boys, Declan and Paul, and went on to adopt two more children, Anthony and Anne.

Their family complete, Jim worked hard to build up his plumbing contractor business while Rose took care of their children at their home in Glasnevin Park. A popular family in the area, they were regulars at the local church and Jim, or Jimmy, as most people knew him, made a name for himself thanks to his cycling prowess.

He could often be seen cycling on his bicycle, heading into the north Dublin countryside for hours at a time. His intense training paid off when he won a couple of national titles, including a Dublin to Galway race.

And when his daughter Rachel went to school in St Mary's in Glasnevin, she took part in every sport she could from basketball to hockey, gymnastics to swimming.

When she was 14, Rachel's family decided to emigrate to Australia. It was the 1980s and Ireland, like most of Europe, was experiencing an uncomfortable economic depression. With the promise of steady work in a country where the cost of living was decidedly lower than Ireland and the weather infinitely better, moving must have seemed like a very attractive alternative to the Callalys.

And although they gave it their best shot, Perth in Western Australia was too far away from the home they missed and so after a year Rose and Jimmy decided to bring their young family back to Ireland.

Their new Dublin home on Collin's Avenue was not far from their original house and the family easily settled back into Irish life.

Rachel returned to St Mary's and resumed her friendships and numerous sporting activities.

The Callalys were always very open with their children about the fact that they were adopted. Rachel was naturally curious about her birth mother and just a few days after she turned 18 years of age, she made it known to the Irish Adoption Board that she would like to be put in touch with her.

It was an emotional reunion between Rachel and her biological mother, Theresa Lowe, who had married and gone on to have four other children, two boys and two girls.

The Lowe family lived in Clondalkin on the south side of the city and Rachel went out to meet them on several occasions, undoubtedly fascinated at how alike she and her birth mother looked.

Though they initially kept in contact for a couple of years, communications between them eventually petered out. It would take almost ten years before they met up again.

✦ ✦ ✦ ✦ ✦

In the meantime, Rachel had her romance with Joe O'Reilly to concentrate on. She was just 17 years old when she first met the dark-haired Dublin man. After leaving school she got a part-time job in Arnotts Department Store on Henry Street.

Almost immediately she caught the eye of Joe, who was then a 19-year-old working in the stores.

'I'd noticed her straight away because she's so tall,' he told me. 'It can be hard finding a tall woman in Ireland.'

In the beginning, Joe did all the running. He overheard her telling a work colleague that she played softball for a local team.

Determined to ask her out on a date, Joe decided to turn up to the softball practice in order to meet her properly. The first night he went she wasn't there, but already smitten Joe did not give up his pursuit and went again the following week.

This time the statuesque blonde was on the pitch, and that evening he asked her if she'd like to go to the cinema with him sometime; she agreed. Joe was impressively tall and somewhat handsome; she was undoubtedly flattered by his efforts to ask her out. He was also a talented sportsman, qualities that are certain to have attracted the athletic Rachel.

At first it was a 'teenager kind of thing,' according to Joe. Rachel was cautious about introducing him to her family and kept things casual. But the relationship soon progressed.

Always one to plan carefully, Rachel insisted they begin to save for the future and Joe was happy to comply, at one stage taking on an extra job at night in a video store to earn more money.

On paper it was a perfect match. They had grown up just a few miles apart, had similar backgrounds, education and aspirations and both had dealt with substantial family issues over the years.

They also shared a love of sports; for years they played on the same softball team and were avid gym goers, keeping weights at their home for those days they couldn't make it out, and worked hard to stay in shape as both were prone to putting on a few pounds if they weren't careful.

They were a handsome couple, Joe as dark as Rachel was fair, and both had friendly, open and easy smiles as the dozens of photographs taken of them together over the twelve years of their relationship can testify.

Joe proposed to Rachel on top of the Eiffel Tower in the springtime of 1994. They waited until they got back to Dublin to buy the engagement ring, which Rachel picked out in Weir's of Grafton Street.

They bought their first home, a modest semi-detached in Santry in north Dublin, two years later, which is when they first moved in together.

And on 4 April 1997 they were married at The Church of the Holy Child in Whitehall, which was followed by a reception at the Shieling Hotel in Raheny. It was a typically big Irish wedding with no expense spared.

Joe and his brother Derek, the best man, wore the full morning attire. The beaming bride looked truly beautiful in her off-the-shoulder ivory gown, complete with veil and flowers entwined in her blonde hair.

They drove to the church and reception in a Bentley car, and the wedding photos show a young and attractive couple, who appear to be deeply in love and obviously excited at the idea of spending the rest of their lives together.

After their two-week honeymoon on Safari in Kenya, the couple returned to their home in Santry.

By this time Joe had left Arnotts and was working in Santry as a team leader at the software company, Oracle. Ambitious and conscientious, he was already on the first step to management.

In the meantime, Rachel was working full-time at a solicitor's office in Donnybrook in south Dublin. And for the first couple of years of their marriage, they worked hard to save for their future family.

They also had a healthy social life; both were members of the same softball team where they made many good friends. And while Joe never drank alcohol, apparently because he never liked the taste of it,

Rachel enjoyed a few glasses of red wine once a week or so with friends, usually in each other's homes.

They were a popular couple. While Rachel was the life and soul of the party who loved a good night of karaoke, Joe was considered quieter and almost gentle. He was also believed to be very kind.

According to a softball team-mate, Bríd Horan, he was always the first to run and grab the first aid kit if someone fell over or hurt themselves on the pitch, always willing to massage a tight muscle or put on a band aid.

'And he'd always have this funny banter and innuendo going on,' she explained.[2] Joe was also a martial arts enthusiast with a black belt in Kempo, and a Star Wars enthusiast who collected memorabilia. He also had a collection of knives.

Another contributor to the apparent success of their marriage was how well they got on with their respective in-laws.

Thanks to a shared love of the movies Joe became close to his brother-in-law Anthony, and the two often went to the cinema together. Rachel regularly visited Joe's sister, Martina, at the residential centre where she lived, bringing her presents, and would always involve her in any family occasions.

Almost three years after they were married, on 10 March 2000, their first son Luke was born. Less than two years later another son, Adam, arrived on 25 October 2001.

The pregnancies were very difficult for Rachel and she was hospitalised for a number of weeks on each occasion. Given how physically strong and healthy she was, her worrying medical issues as she waited to give birth came as a surprise to the couple. As Joe admitted later: 'It runs you down.'

Thankfully the actual labours for both boys went well and the O'Reillys were delighted with their two babies, who Rachel doted over. With her inherent maternal instincts and caring nature, she was a natural mother who put her children before everything.

Career wise, things were going from strength to strength for Joe. In 2002, shortly after the birth of his second son, he landed a managerial position with Viacom, an outdoor advertising company. His new office was based in the Bluebell Industrial Estate, and it proved to be quite a promotion as Joe was now in charge of 26 employees. His job was to co-ordinate the company's bill-posters division, which placed ads on the sides of buses or on hoardings in train stations.

He also had to check up on their work, which involved going out to stations and bus depots to make sure advertisements had been placed.

Some friends believe the deterioration in Joe and Rachel's relationship coincided with his new appointment.

A friend of the couple's, Paula Carney, told how soon after he joined he started to disappear on overnight bus inspections to Limerick and Cork.

She had a friend who worked for Viacom, often as late as 10pm. Asked why Joe would be doing overnight inspections, the friend replied, 'He doesn't.'

It's difficult to know if Rachel began to notice any warning signs. Friends say she was very private and was intent on behaving as though everything was fine with her home life.

'Rachel wanted to create a picture of a happy pixie family, the house in the country, the nice lifestyle, and the 2.4 children,' explained her friend Bríd Horan. [3]

Besides, she was constantly busy. As well as bringing up her two boys, at this stage more or less on her own, she had her sporting commitments. She played softball every week and hockey with a team based at her old school. She also continued to work one night a week at the solicitor's office and was selling Avon products to generate extra income.

By 2003, she decided it was time to move to somewhere more suitable for her boys to grow up.

The housing estate in Santry had become a little more crowded and noisy since they had first moved there and besides, she had always dreamt of living somewhere with lots of room and possibly a sea view.

At the time, Joe claimed to be too busy at his new job to help her look for a new home, and so she house-hunted on her own while looking after her two babies.

For years her father Jimmy had been cycling around the north Dublin countryside and had always mentioned the village of Naul as a beautiful and quiet spot, which was just twenty minutes from her family home on Collins' Avenue.

To Rachel it sounded like an ideal area. Strapping the two kids in the car, she followed the directions given to her by Jimmy and began to regularly drive around Naul in search of anything suitable.

Beldarragh is a small townland in Naul, tucked away off the old Dublin to Belfast Road. It can be difficult to find if you don't know the landmarks. The most obvious is Murphy's Quarry, a busy mine that sees a steady stream of trucks and lorries using the narrow roads to and from the main motorways.

Less than a mile from the entrance of the Quarry, following a pot-holed ribbon of a road up a slight hill, Rachel found Lambay View.

It was a pretty three-bedroom bungalow and was in need of some attention but boasted a massive garden, and if you stretched and stood on your tippy-toes you could see the sea.

She brought Joe out to see the property and he agreed they should make a bid for the house. With the help of the solicitor she worked for, she got things sorted, as usual, in double-quick time.

Rachel's friends and family remember her being delighted with her new home. She quickly set about getting to know her neighbours; within weeks of moving in she ordered Joe out to buy a barbecue for a party she threw to help introduce them to the local community.

She continued selling her Avon products and took on Tupperware items as well, not only to make money but also to meet new people living around the area.

Rachel threw herself into community life with gusto and when there was opposition in the area to the erection of a telephone mast, she got involved with the protest. She even went on the radio station, *Newstalk 106*, to voice her concerns.

The mast, based at Murphy's Quarry, was put up regardless.

In between all her various projects, Rachel was also trying to get the actual house in order. Luckily, considering Joe was around less and less, she had her family to help out with the jobs that needed doing.

Her father Jimmy and her brother Paul, who was working for Jimmy's plumbing company at the time, offered their services, as did her birth-brother Thomas Lowe, a carpenter by trade.

Rachel and her birth family, the Lowes, had met up again, after ten years of almost no contact, when Joe bumped into her sister Sandra Lowe at Jackie Skelly's Gym in Park West. Sandra, who is very similar in looks to Rachel, spotted Joe at the gym shortly after he first joined.

'I was working in a gym in Clondalkin at the time and a colleague of mine was showing him around and I noticed him,' Sandra explained later. [4]

'And I said to myself: "God, that's Joe." Rachel and Joe had been dating back when she first got in contact and I remembered him.

'So I said it to mum first and then the next time he was there I went over to him and he couldn't believe that it was me because he hadn't seen me in years. He organised a meeting in their house and we met the kids and it was amazing.'

This time, Rachel was determined to have some kind of steady relationship with her birth family and she regularly organised shopping trips with Theresa and Sandra. After a few months she also became close to Thomas, who stayed over at the house in Naul a couple of times and helped put up their decking in the back garden.

From the outside, Rachel's life was flourishing. Her sons loved their new schools and they had plenty of kids in the area to play with, while Rachel had made loads of new friends and loved her new home.

But her relationship with Joe was hitting the rocks and though she refused to confide in her family, obviously not wishing to upset or worry them and perhaps out of loyalty to her husband, she acknowledged on a couple of occasions to friends that she had concerns.

Her close pals had already noticed that Joe was not around as much as he used to be. He had even insisted that he and Rachel join different softball teams, arguing that they would not have to pay a babysitter if they took turns to mind the kids.

And more often than not he was sleeping in the spare room. He told others that it was a mid-week thing, done out of courtesy to Rachel because he didn't want to wake her with his early starts. He also complained that their youngest son Adam had a habit, like most young children his age, of climbing into their bed in the middle of the night.

They had also argued about having another child. Rachel desperately wanted a girl to complete her family but Joe refused; he said he was happy with his two sons and didn't see the need for another child.

In October 2003, Joe decided to go on a softball trip to Florida—even though it meant he missed Rachel's 30th birthday.

The couple's mutual friend Celine Keogh, spent the evening with Rachel and helped her celebrate; it was one of the first times she voiced her concerns about her marriage. Rachel asked her friend if she thought Joe was having an affair; Celine said she didn't think so. Rachel also spoke to Celine about how there was little affection in her marriage.

'She'd say she couldn't remember the last time she'd kissed Joe or the last time they'd had sex, that their beds were like musical chairs,' Celine explained. 'One would get in and the other would get out.' [5]

In the meantime, Joe was telling friends and anyone else who would listen that he wasn't 'getting any at home'—something most of them knew he was responsible for.

By May 2004, the difficulties in Rachel's marriage were taking their toll and she developed the painful skin condition psoriasis around her eyes, on her arms and between her fingers.

For all intents and purposes, she was bringing up the kids on her own. Joe was staying over at his office twice a week, claiming it was handier to get to softball practice.

Even when he did stay at home he woke at 6am, apparently to go to the gym before he went into work. It was usually late evening before he arrived home.

Rumours of an affair began to circulate, but according to Rachel's childhood friend, Jackie Connor, she dismissed them most of the time.

'She laughed it off,' Jackie told a reporter. 'And said: "Why would he have an affair when he isn't interested in sex?"'

Jackie also confirmed that Joe was not pulling his weight in the house. 'Rachel did everything in the house, from the DIY, to the accounts to the parenting,' she said. [6]

'The only thing he ever did was burn the rubbish. I'd have seen Joe about five times in the last year. He was absent from the family, definitely from January 2004. She didn't have a family life.'

It was despicable behaviour that included calling Rachel names like 'the Dragon' to her friends or roaring at her on the softball pitch in front of everyone, causing tears to well in her eyes.

There was also a night when the couple was supposed to finally go out for dinner together to celebrate her 30th birthday, eight months after the event.

Her girlfriends remember how she was giddily excited about the evening. Like any woman looking forward to a date she planned carefully what she would wear and discussed with friends the kind of jewellery that would complement her outfit.

But when they rang her after the weekend, she had to tell them how Joe had cancelled at the last minute. He said he had been called into the office—on a Friday night. She was heartbroken.

But perhaps the most hurtful thing to happen to the doting mother was when she was 'anonymously reported' to the social services for being rough with her children.

She was distraught and confused at being asked to defend her mothering skills in front of a social worker in early June 2004. Friends described her youngest boy, Adam, as 'the Velcro child' who couldn't bear to be away from his mother's side. His big brother Luke 'idolised his mammy and was the spitting image of her.'

While Joe was apparently open about how he no longer loved Rachel, it is impossible to know when—if ever—she stopped loving him.

Despite his cruel conduct, some friends believe Rachel 'idolised' her husband right up until just a few months before her death.

Her mother Rose thought Rachel remained loyal to Joe until the morning she died.

'She loved Joe, she would have looked over anything that made him look bad,' Rose said.[7]

'I think up to the end she still loved him but then love is blind.'

Jackie Connor, however, believes Rachel's feelings towards her husband had changed over the summer of 2004, especially after a massive argument between them she witnessed at the house in Naul.

Rachel later told her best friend that she didn't love Joe anymore but that she would try and make it work for the kids.

There was also 'definite tension about an affair,' according to Jackie.

'There were rumours and she was questioning him a lot. She had laughed it off but I think she had a long hard think.

'I was in Eddie Rockets with her and the boys about nine days before 4 October [the day she was killed] and she told me she did give him an ultimatum. He had gone off to England and she'd spoken to him on the phone. There were to be no more late night inspections, he was to spend more time at home.' [8]

But things didn't change for Rachel; in fact they just got worse and, on Friday, 1 October she rang another friend, Paula Carney.

'She was very upset, very depressed. She said she was putting on weight and that she needed to speak to me, that things weren't great at home,' she said later.

It's hard to know what else Rachel went through over that last weekend of her life.

The last time she saw Jackie was on the Friday morning when her friend called in after coming off a night-shift from work. She later said Rachel seemed okay, possibly a little tired after staying up late to watch the television the night before.

She played a hockey match on the Saturday morning in which she was injured but when a team-mate rang the following morning she said she felt fine.

But there was a dreadful row that Sunday night.

Apparently Rachel finally confronted her husband about his affair after she heard her children mention 'daddy's friend Nikki'.

As usual Joe slept in the spare room that night and got up early the following morning. Leaving the house at around 5.40am, he made his way to the gym for a quick work-out before heading to the office.

A couple of hours later Rachel was awake, undoubtedly tired and upset by the clash she had the night before with her husband.

But as far as Rachel knew, that Monday was going to be like any other day: the boys had to be taken care of and there were jobs and duties to do.

CHAPTER 2

Murder in the Naul

THE MORNING OF 4 October 2004 was a crisp, clear and sunny; it was a beautiful autumn day—the kind that shows the countryside in Naul off to perfection.

Rachel, always energetic and with a daily to-do list as long as her arm, probably crossed over the hallway into the bedroom her sons shared, and quickly roused them. Getting Luke and Adam ready for school was an intense operation. Rachel also had a delivery of Avon and Tupperware products to make that day to a customer who lived two or three miles away.

Then, before she knew it, it would be time to pick up Adam again from his crèche at 12.30pm. Thankfully it was her friend Michelle Mulligan's turn to collect Luke and her own kids from school that day. It was a godsend of an arrangement they had sorted out two or three months earlier; Rachel would collect the youngsters on Tuesdays and Thursdays while Michelle had volunteered to do it Mondays, Wednesdays and Fridays.

Strapping her two little boys into her car, Rachel undoubtedly noticed, not for the first time, that the vehicle needed a serious clean-out. Sweet wrappers, bits of clothing and plastic bags were strewn around the floor and seats.

But there always seemed to be something more pressing to be done—bringing the boys to a birthday party, going for a picnic, softball practice, a night out with friends or catching up with her family; things that were far more important than tackling a car with a vacuum cleaner.

It had rained the night before and the roads around Rachel's home were still slightly wet, but the strong sunshine was doing its best to dry them out.

First to drop off was Luke, who had started junior infants four weeks earlier at the Hedgestown primary school, just five miles outside Lusk Village.

Leaving Adam still strapped securely into his seat, Rachel took Luke's hand and walked him in through the gates. She made her way to the classroom and had a brief conversation with his teacher Áine Doyle. She then returned to her car and set off towards Tots United Montessori School with her youngest son Adam.

Already there waiting at the door of the school, just after 9.25am, were the mothers of some of the other pupils, Cathy Henry, Paula Matthews and Naomi Gargan. In a hurry to get back and make her deliveries, Rachel just said a friendly hello to the women. She kissed her son goodbye, told him she'd see him later and walked back to her car.

'Her car turned left in the direction of her house,' Cathy Henry later told gardaí. 'That was the last I saw of her.'

The local milkman, who has worked the same round for the last 22 years, spotted her car back outside her house that morning at around 10am, just like usual.

He noticed, however, that the curtains were pulled, which was not normal.

Helen Moore, who runs the local Montessori school, knew Rachel well. Luke had already attended the school the year before and Adam had started there that September.

School finished every day at 12.30pm and Rachel was always there to pick her son up at exactly the right time. But by 12.45pm there was still no sign of her and no message to say she was running late.

Puzzled, Helen rang the O'Reilly's home number; there was no answer so she left a message. When she tried Rachel's mobile phone it just rang out to her message minder.

After trying both phones a few times, Helen decided to ring Joe and went through her records to find his number. By this stage it was 1.10pm.

'I made contact with him on a mobile phone and told him Rachel hadn't arrived to pick Adam up,' she later explained, 'He said he was eating his lunch and it was unusual that she didn't pick up Adam, he then said he was just going to make a phone call.'[1]

A short time later, Joe rang the teacher back to say he was on his way to collect Adam. He arrived about 2.05pm.

'He was smartly dressed; I just brought Adam to the door,' Helen said.

'He appeared grand, but flushed in the face when he arrived. I just passed Adam over to him and I reminded him that Luke was over in Hedgestown school and had to be collected at 2pm or 2.15pm and to collect him perhaps on the journey.'

When Joe had hung up, he called his brother-in-law, Anthony Callaly.

At the time Anthony was still living at home and was helping his father to paint the exterior of the house when his mobile phone rang; Joe's number flashed up on the little screen.

'He sounded agitated and the first thing he asked me was if Rachel was in the house. I said she wasn't, and then checked with my mother and father and my two brothers,' Anthony later explained. [2]

'I checked on the roadway for her car then I told Joe that Rachel hadn't been to the house all morning.

'I asked why and he said she hadn't collected Adam from school. I just said to keep trying her mobile and asked him when the last time they'd been in contact was. He said he'd been calling her all morning but to no avail, it just kept going to her voice mail.

'It was very unusual she hadn't collected her son, she lived her life for her kids.

'I tried calling her several times but it just kept going to her voice mail. My mother left a message asking her to contact us. My mother then offered to go out to the house to see if she'd fallen or was incapacitated.

'I phoned Joe back and told him we hadn't made contact on the landline or the mobile, he just said to keep trying.

'My father asked me to contact Joe again to see if there was a neighbour who could check the house. He replied with Sarah Harmon's number.'

Rachel's mother Rose had been in the kitchen making lunch for her husband and three sons when Joe's phone call was answered by Anthony. She immediately sensed there was something wrong. It was totally out of character for Rachel not to have picked her son up.

'I was at the cooker and he [Anthony] asked me had I heard or seen from Rachel,' she later explained to the gardaí. 'I asked why? What was the problem? And he told me she hadn't turned up at the crèche.

'I knew it was very unusual for Adam to still be at the crèche and there being no word from Rachel. I rang her mobile, as far as I can remember it was switched on and it rang, I left a message to say this is your mum and to ring me back, I left a similar message on the landline. It was roughly 1.20pm.

'As soon as I put down the phone I was very concerned and I said to my husband that I felt there was something wrong, I said I was going out [to Rachel's], as long as the traffic is moving it only takes about twenty minutes.'

Rose drove straight to her daughter's home and immediately spotted her daughter's car parked 'as always at the end of the driveway.'

'The front door was very seldom used,' Rose later explained.[3]

'I always went to the back and to the patio doors. The curtains were drawn, which was very, very unusual, I'd never seen them drawn before.'

Feeling even more anxious than before, Rose quickly walked into the kitchen where she noticed the sink tap was 'on and was running very strongly.'

'I went over to the utility room calling Rachel's name as I was going, I went through the kitchen door and the sitting room door. The cabinet doors were open and stuff was scattered on the floor, I felt very uneasy.

'I walked out into the hall all the while calling Rachel's name, I went straight down to the end to the boy's room—everything looked normal so I walked out of there. Rachel's room is directly opposite and I sort of looked in, then I noticed Rachel lying on the floor.'

It was a sight no mother should ever have to witness—her daughter's lifeless body stretched out on the floor, her blonde hair completely matted and her head covered in so much blood that it had stuck to the floor.

'The blood looked like jam,' Rose explained later. 'It was thick and congealed and a beetroot colour.'

She said it looked as though Rachel had fallen, her head was towards the door, almost reaching the threshold while her feet were back into the room. But Rose did not believe there was an innocent explanation.

'As soon as I saw her I knew she was dead,' Rose said. 'I knew she was murdered, I remember talking to her and rubbing her arms, they were so cold.'

In a blind panic Rose went in search of a phone to call for help. After a few minutes she came across a mobile.

'I picked up the phone, I didn't know how to use it,' she said. 'I kept pushing numbers and eventually a man answered. I told him I needed help: "I think my daughter's dead." To this day I still don't know who that man was.'

It was shortly after this frantic and garbled phone call that Rachel's nearest neighbour and friend, Sarah Harmon arrived. She had been contacted after Jimmy Callaly asked if there was a neighbour who could check on the house.

Rose brought Sarah down the corridor to her daughter's body.

'I told her: "I think Rachel is dead". As far as I remember she didn't touch Rachel, she got very upset and walked back into the kitchen and rang the emergency services.'

Sarah, herself a mother of two who became friendly with Rachel shortly after the O'Reillys moved to Naul, remembers getting to the house around 2.15pm.

'I saw Rachel lying in the doorway of the bedroom,' she later said.[4]

'I didn't recognise her facially; blood was covering her hair and face.

'I put my hand on her back. I was requested by the paramedic to check for a pulse, I could find none.'

Other people then began to arrive at the scene; first was Michelle Mulligan who had collected Luke from school as arranged and was dropping him off. Pulling in behind her car was Joe, who had gone to collect his other son Adam.

Rose came out of the house to meet them in the driveway.

'I looked behind her [Michelle Mulligan] and Joe O'Reilly was there,' Rose said. 'And he smiled at me.'

Rose told her son-in-law to hurry into the house, that something was wrong with Rachel. He ran past her, into the kitchen and down the hallway to the bedroom.

While Joe would later say that he embraced Rachel's body, Rose remembers it differently.

'To my recollection the only thing he done was put his two fingers on her neck,' she said later adding: 'He said to her; "Jesus Rachel, What did you do?" Even then I thought it was bizarre. Strange, I remember thinking it was strange at the time. Then he got up and put his hand to his head, he seemed to be upset.' [5]

Rachel's best friend since childhood, Jackie Connor, then arrived. A neurosurgical nurse, she had just finished eight days of continuous twelve hour shifts and was at her Santry home in bed sleeping when Joe rang her a little earlier that afternoon.

It was Jackie's birthday that day and Joe later explained that he rang to see if Rachel had called in on her friend.

'He said: "Happy birthday, is Rachel there with you?"

'I said: "No, I'd been asleep,"' she later explained. [6]

'We [Jackie and Rachel] had made arrangements that if she was in the area she would drop off a suitcase and a hedge trimmer, she had a key for my house so she could let herself in.

'I checked downstairs, he [Joe] told me she hadn't collected the kids. We were on the phone for a couple of minutes and he said he was driving home from work.'

Jackie went back to bed but could only manage a fitful, short sleep.

'I was worried something had happened to Rachel,' she explained.

'I rang her at home and on the mobile but there was no reply.' She dressed quickly and jumped into her car.

'I drove over to her house and kept my eyes open,' she said.

'I was worried she'd had an accident. It was very unusual for her not to pick up the boys.

'I got to the house about 2.20pm and I went to the back door of the house and went into the kitchen, Joe O'Reilly was there, Mrs Callaly and Sarah Harmon. Joe said to me to go down and see if I could do something, he told me she [Rachel] was in the bedroom.

'They were all in shock and it was clear something terrible had happened.'

In the course of her training and work as a nurse, Jackie would have seen her fair share of grisly sights. But nothing could have prepared her for seeing her own best friend so badly beaten.

'I saw Rachel's body lying in the door of the bedroom,' she said.

'There was a lot of blood everywhere, a lot of congealed blood and there was a gash on the right-hand side of her head, over her right ear, it was very noticeable.

'I checked for a pulse, her hand was very cold, there was no pulse so I checked her neck, checked her right pupil but it was fixed and dilated. I couldn't turn her over [into the recovery position] she was very heavy and stiff. The room was very dark, the curtains were pulled.

'There was blood all around the doorframe and hall, splatters high up and down low. I told him [Joe] Rachel was dead, went up to the kitchen and washed my hands, there were a lot of splashes on the sink.' [7]

The small shell-shocked group stood helplessly in the kitchen, all they could do now was wait for the emergency services to arrive.

Jimmy Callaly had called his wife several times to see what was happening and she had told him to get help, that she thought Rachel was dead. Paul Callaly, another of Rachel's three brothers, immediately rang for an ambulance and explained how they could find the O'Reilly home. He then drove himself and his father out to the house in Naul.

Rose had also rung for an ambulance as did Joe who told the emergency services operator that there was blood all over the walls and CDs 'all over the place'.

Believing that it sounded like a possible scene of a crime, the operator told Joe to get out of the room and not to let anyone else in.

Paramedics with the HSE ambulance services, Michael Cardiff and Frank Rice, arrived at the house and were brought down to Rachel's body by Rose and Joe.

'The upper torso was twisted up, the legs were in the opposite direction, it was an awkward position,' Michael Cardiff later explained. [8]

'There were no signs of life. It was totally suspicious because of the trauma to the deceased and the amount of blood. It was splattered on the doorways etc, we told everyone to stay out of the room.'

His colleague Frank Rice told how the room where Rachel's body lay was very dark and it was difficult to see.

'I don't think the light was working, we had to get a flashlight,' he said. 'There was a massive blow to the right-hand side of the head. I put an ECG on her, it measures electricity from the heart, and there was no electricity activity whatsoever, which means the heart is not working.'

The rest of Rachel's family began to arrive, led by her distressed father Jimmy and brother Paul.

'There were ambulance men and police men,' said Jimmy. [9]

'I walked up to the house, went as far as the hallway but a ban garda stopped me, she said don't go up to the room so I didn't go up to the room.

'She ushered me into the front room but I couldn't stay in there, I was very claustrophobic, I had to get out. I was very upset. The ambulance man said: "Come out and sit in the ambulance". So that's what I done.'

Rachel's other two brothers, Anthony and Declan also drove out.

'On my way out to the house Paul had rung me to say Rachel was dead,' said Anthony.

'I tried to run in [into the house] to see Rachel but gardaí stopped me.

'They [his parents] were there with Joe, everyone was very emotional … all crying.'

Eventually the distraught Callaly family were persuaded that there was nothing more they could do, that Rachel was gone and the gardaí now had to take over and preserve the scene if they were to have any chance of finding out what had happened to her.

In disbelief and crushing grief, they headed southwards to their home. For all of them it was to be the first of countless sleepless nights as they tried to rid their imaginations of what could have happened to Rachel in her final moments.

Joe helped his two frightened and confused young sons into his car and headed northwards to his mother's house in Louth. Whether or not he slept that night is anybody's guess.

CHAPTER 3

The Immediate Aftermath

IN THE DAYS after Rachel's murder it was assumed by most that she had been the victim of a burglary gone horribly wrong. After all, who would want to deliberately kill this sociable housewife and devoted mum who loved sports and the odd glass or two of wine?

Two days after the murder, *The Evening Herald* newspaper ran a front page story, just one of many, revealing it was believed Rachel had been killed at around 10am, shortly after she had dropped her sons off at their schools. Other stories that appeared in the press speculated she had been beaten with either her own hockey stick or softball bat.

There were also initial reports that gardaí thought she may have fallen prey to a criminal gang from the north inner city, which had been linked to a spate of robberies in north Dublin.

It was claimed gardaí thought this gang had been cruising the area looking for a likely target and spotting the isolated O'Reilly home, found it to be empty. But

Rachel returned from dropping her boys to school and surprised the burglars who in turn panicked and attacked her before making their escape.

But when the garda crime scene team (CST) carried out their examination of the house they did not find a single suspicious drop of blood, a strand of hair, a piece of fibre or any other kind of DNA sample.

Surely in the struggle between Rachel and her attacker, something from the killer would have been left behind? But the house was forensically clean.

Thanks to the popularity of American cop shows such as *CSI* and *Law and Order*, never before has there been such interest or 'armchair expertise' in what happens at the scene of a crime.

And while the reality in Ireland is a little less glamorous and a lot more time-consuming than what's portrayed in a weekly television series, it's true to say that the work of these men and women is of an extraordinarily intricate nature and often leads directly to the capture and charging of the perpetrator of a crime.

Once the call comes through that a 'suspicious death' has occurred, the crime scene team is quickly assembled.

The team includes a fingerprint expert, a ballistics expert, a photographer, a mapper (who does not always travel with the rest of the team) and a crime scene manager.

No matter where the 'suspicious death' takes place, the CST always travels from its headquarters in Dublin. So while it may take five hours to get to a remote part of Donegal, they would have arrived at the murder scene at Naul in north Dublin within half-an-hour.

Travelling in specific vans that hold the equipment they will need to examine and gather evidence, they can also change into their specialised protective hooded suits, made of a particular material that prevents them from contaminating the scene.

A familiar sight on the television news, their clothing is bright white and they wear gloves, masks and footsies, leaving nothing to chance.

On their way to a scene the team will gather as much information as possible about the crime that has taken place by contacting the local garda force, which will already be at the location and, by the time they arrive, the scene will have been preserved and cordoned off.

During a normal investigation, the first to enter the scene is the photographer who will take photographs and film the scene. Getting as many photographs as possible is imperative because reference could be made to something at the scene later on during the case.

Once the photographer is finished, the ballistics and fingerprints experts enter the scene. Working hand-in-hand they examine every surface, searching for evidence, be it a fingerprint, a hair or a fibre.

One of the first things they will do is build a path to the body, which allows them and the pathologist to make their way to and from the body without disturbing any evidence.

Following the examination, the only fingerprints the experts found in the bedroom were those of Joe, Rachel and her mother Rose. And the only blood other than Rachel's found at the scene was on the washing machine in the utility room.

Tests showed that it belonged to Rachel's birth brother, Thomas Lowe, who later explained to gardaí how he had cut himself while building a deck in the garden.

He bandaged himself up but dripped blood onto the floor and washing machine while getting plasters from a first aid box in the utility room.

So despite Rachel's violent death there had been nothing left at the scene, apart from DNA evidence from those who had already admitted touching Rachel as she lay on the floor, like Joe and Rose.

But as the gardaí will tell you, often what you don't find is every bit as important as what you do find.

And in this murder case the gardaí had to acknowledge that the absence of anyone else's fingerprints strongly pointed to the killer being one of the people whose prints were found at the scene.

As well as gathering evidence, the CST examines the body of the victim and a pathologist will also attend the scene, usually arriving around the same time.

Dr Marie Cassidy, the State Pathologist, visually examined Rachel and took a series of temperatures from her body in an attempt to determine a rough time of death.

More than one-hundred samples were collected from Rachel, those who had come into contact with her and from the room where she was killed. They were then passed on to forensic scientist, Dr Diane Daly from the State's Forensic Science Laboratory, who examined them for any kind of evidence that might help them discover the identity of the killer.

And while this intense garda investigation continued, interest in the murder of a young woman in her isolated home on the outskirts of Dublin intensified.

Rachel's body was finally released back to her family, and the night before the funeral the Callaly family invited all of her friends and extended family over to their home at Collins' Avenue.

It was an emotional evening, with people swapping fond memories, speculating who could have killed her and wondering as well as worrying about the future of her two little boys.

Earlier that day Rachel's sister Anne and her sister-in-law Denise had gone shopping to find clothes for Rachel to wear in the coffin. They had settled on a casual combination of combat trousers and a top. Rachel, it was well known, had little time for fashion and had never been one to dress up.

And as distraught friends, neighbours and family sat around the Callalys, drinking tea and sharing their shock at what had happened, it was suggested that those who wanted to write a farewell letter or note to Rachel could do so that night and then place it in the coffin.

It was a popular proposal and most of those gathered went off to find a quiet spot to sit down and compose their own personal thoughts and prayers for Rachel.

Jimmy and Rose Callaly made their way to their conservatory and were joined for a short time by Joe.

But he soon got up and went to the kitchen to write his last letter to his wife.

He had a short conversation with Rachel's friend Jackie Connor about what he should write.

'I told him I'd spent an hour writing a letter,' she would later explain. [1]

'He got a paper and pen, sat down at the Callaly's table and wrote his letter.

'I had bought a box of cigarettes for Rachel because I knew she liked her "sneaky cigarettes" as she called them. A lot of people wrote notes.'

Joe also placed the letter he had written to Rachel into her coffin.

Rachel's funeral mass took place the following day, 11 October 2004, at The Holy Child Church in Whitehall, close to where she had grown up.

Poignantly placed on top of Rachel's coffin was a piece of paper with the word 'Mammy' written on it. There was also a Tweetie-pie cuddly toy.

It was an intensely emotional day and as Joe walked towards the pulpit to give his oration at the end of the Mass, sobs could be heard echoing around the church.

In a steady voice, he spoke of his life with Rachel and described the joy and happiness she had brought to him and others. He told the large congregation how their eldest son looked incredibly like his mother. That every time he looked into Luke's eyes, he could see the wife he loved. And he told them that their younger son, Adam, had the good-natured cheek and positive attitude of Rachel.

He spoke of her sporting prowess in hockey, swimming and softball and told the gathered mourners how she had travelled to many countries despite being so young when she died.

He also referred to how she had achieved the personal goals she had set herself: getting married, having children, living in the country, having a sea view and having lots of friends.

Looking at the devastated faces of his wife's family and friends, Joe said: 'Mission accomplished, Rachel, well done,' and then thanked her for her love and for making him laugh. 'See you on the other side,' he added. 'We all thank you. Bye for now.'

But before he stepped down, Joe told the congregation he wanted to say a few words to 'the person responsible' for Rachel's death.

'Unlike you, she is at peace; unlike you, she is sleeping,' he declared. 'She forgives you. And I hope she gives me the strength some day to forgive you.'

Yet despite these powerful and public words, people were already wondering at his rather strange reaction to the brutal death of his wife.

Rachel's father Jimmy admitted later that although he tried to ignore it, he noticed how Joe was behaving very differently to the rest of the family at Rachel's funeral.

'He was out the back talking to people, laughing and joking and that,' Jimmy explained. 'And other people said to me that it was very odd, the way he was talking and carrying on. We were that upset, we weren't taking it in. [2]

'We were sympathising, putting our arms around him—we were that upset. He said a few odd things himself and I was saying to myself: "That's shock, people react differently to shock."

'But he wasn't acting like a grieving husband. It didn't seem to affect him the way it affected us. He was sort of normal.'

Rachel's body was buried at Fingal Cemetery in Balgriffin in north Dublin. The funeral party met up again at the Regency Hotel afterwards for a reception.

Joe was involved in several conversations about her killing that friends later described as 'inappropriate' and 'upsetting.'

'I went to leave with friends and on the way out I saw Joe O'Reilly sitting with his mother, his sister and her boyfriend,' Fiona Slevin, a good friend of Rachel's, later explained. [3]

'He asked me to stay, that he hadn't spoken to me yet, so I stayed till 6pm. There was a discussion about the murder weapon. He [Joe] said: "I don't know why they're searching in the fields, it's in the water."

'I was shocked and his reaction then was like he'd said something wrong. And he said: "If I'd done it that's where it would be, because there's water all around and it would get rid of DNA and all that sort of stuff."'

Rachel's childhood friend, Tara Kennedy, was also disturbed by a chat she had with Joe.

'We had various conversations but something stuck in my mind,' she later explained. [4]

'He said: "It's ironic, here we were at the church at 10am and she had been killed at 10.05am and here we are at 2pm [at the reception] when the body was found at 2.10pm."

'I felt shocked at these words, I just remember looking at my feet. I just lifted my head and went on to change the subject to Star Wars. I knew that Star Wars was a big hobby of his, I knew he had a room dedicated to Star Wars in the house. I just wanted to change the subject.'

Immediately after the funeral the gardaí issued a fresh appeal for taxi drivers, hackney drivers and delivery drivers who were in the Beldarragh area on the morning of the murder to contact them.

They told how the murder weapon had still not been found but that they were continuing to search the fields around the house and were investigating any known criminals who might have been in the area on that day.

But behind the scenes gardaí had begun in earnest to look much closer to the O'Reilly home.

The botched burglary theory disintegrated almost immediately. Even Rose had told how she believed the crime scene looked 'contrived,' as though somebody wanted it to look as if the place had been broken into.

And why had €860 placed in a container in the utility room been left behind and over €400 left untouched in Rachel's handbag?

Surely a thief would have fled the scene with something more than just a video camera bag and a satchel with a jewellery box in it, both of which were found the day after the murder less than half a mile from the house.

The gardaí later claimed that even these items, which were confirmed to belong to the O'Reilly's, looked as though they had been placed in the ditch to be found rather than dumped in a panic.

A huge investigation team, up to seventy-strong at stages, began to comb the area and question local farmers and neighbours if they had seen anything suspicious that day.

Nobody had spotted anyone fleeing the scene and the murder weapon was nowhere to be found in the local vicinity. But rather than this being a set-back, the gardaí claimed later, it actually helped them to narrow down their investigation.

So brutal was the attack on Rachel that the gardaí believed whoever had killed her must have been covered in her blood. If it had been a burglar he would have immediately made his escape. But there was no trail of blood from the house and nobody had been seen speeding away.

The evidence so far showed that this had been a calm killer, one who had possibly showered thoroughly after killing Rachel and taken the towels he had used to dry himself, along with the murder weapon, and deposited them far away from the house.

This was beginning to show all the signs of a meticulously planned murder.

And the first piece of evidence to firmly point them in Joe's direction was a statement from Michelle Slattery, a receptionist at Viacom, where Joe worked, who told them Joe had arrived back into the office that day at about noon.

She noticed straight away that his face was puffy and bloated and his eyes were the same.

'There were a few things, but Michelle Slattery's observations spoke volumes,' a senior officer on the case later confirmed. [5]

'We were also suspicious of the items that had been found in the ditch. The camcorder had Joe O'Reilly's name on it and as a result wouldn't have been worth anything to a burglar.

'It wouldn't be something a robber would take because of the identity on it but he reckoned it was ideal because it would be so easily found and traced back to him.'

On the night of the murder, three garda officers had called out to Joe's mother's house in Dunleer in Co. Louth.

They were greeted at the door by Joe's mother, Ann, and ushered into the sitting room. A few minutes later Joe appeared from upstairs where he had been comforting his boys and putting them to bed.

During the hour-long meeting the officers asked Joe about his movements that day and if he had been experiencing any marital problems.

He played the role of a grieving widower impeccably, according to the gardaí. Always calm and measured in his replies to any of their questions, he appeared to be honest and willing to help them in any way he could.

He claimed that things had been rocky between him and Rachel for a while but everything was OK in more recent times.

There was one major slip-up, however, when he denied that he had cheated on Rachel. The officers asked him twice and he told them no, that he had not had an affair. But when they asked for a third time, he obviously thought he had better come clean.

He admitted to seeing a former work colleague, Nikki Pelley, but claimed the relationship had never been that serious and was over. He said he had initially lied about it because he didn't want his family to know.

He then detailed his movements that morning from when he left the house at 5.40am to meeting his work colleague Derek Quearney at the gym to going to his office and then leaving again to carry out a bus inspection at the Broadstone depot in central Dublin between 9.30am and 11.30am.

Later that night Quearney was contacted and confirmed Joe's version of events to the best of his recollection. Joe now had an alibi.

A week or so later, Joe and Rachel's parents agreed to be interviewed on RTE's television news at lunchtime.

The three sat together on the sofa in the Callaly's sitting room. Joe was so close to his mother-in-law that their knees were touching. They took it in turns to speak and swapped encouraging looks as they described how they had found Rachel's body. They appealed for anyone with any information to come forward.

Their next television appearance, just over a week later, was very different.

Joe and Rose were interviewed on the *Late Late Show* on 22 October 2004. It was obvious Rose's attitude towards her son-in-law had changed.

Where just days before Rose had sat close to Joe, looking at him directly as he spoke, the frostiness between the pair was now palpable. Sitting in two large arm chairs just a few inches apart, placed so they could face the host and the audience, Rose held herself stiffly, with her hands folded in her lap and directed all her conversation to Kenny.

And whenever Joe spoke, rather than looking at him, she stared straight out into the audience to where her husband Jimmy, daughter Anne and Rachel's friend and neighbour, Sarah Harmon were sitting together.

It was a tense interview, not only because of the heartbreaking subject matter, but because of the stony-faced expression Rose wore throughout.

In contrast, Joe leaned forward, eager to answer Kenny's questions, cracking a slight joke or two, and giving the impression to some that he was almost enjoying being under the bright lights of a television studio.

A limousine had been sent by the station to pick them up from Collins' Avenue earlier that day and the small group had travelled together to the studio, for what must have been a truly nerve racking experience.

Joe, however, seemed to be taking the appearance in his stride and while backstage in the hospitality lounge the Callalys were somewhat taken aback at his casual manner with other guests and ability to 'wolf back' sandwiches, while they sat silently waiting to tell the country of their heartbreak at Rachel's murder.

When it came to the actual interview Rose, as always, handled herself with dignity and gave measured and articulate answers to any questions asked.

She told how her energetic daughter had been 'a bolt of lightning from the time she could move.'

And as she described the awful details of the day she found her Rachel's battered body, her voice softened. 'I was the one who found her,' she confirmed.

'I went up to the bedroom and to my dying day, I'll never forget the scene that met me.

'Pat she had a horrific death,' Rose said and beside her Joe dropped his eyes and pursed his lips.

The presenter turned to the Callaly family members sitting in the audience and asked Rachel's sister, who was visibly upset, what kind of woman she had been.

'She was such an amazing person, a natural nurturer, a fantastic sister, a super wife, a fantastic daughter,' Anne replied. 'She touched so many people's lives … we're so devastated by this.'

And Sarah, the woman who was the second person at the scene of Rachel's death, told the *Late Late Show* viewers: 'There's no replacing Rachel for anybody here or for her boys.'

Stifling a sob she was comforted by the victim's father Jimmy, who put his arm around her.

Joe spoke at length during the emotional interview, explaining how he had arrived back at his home to be told by Rose that she thought Rachel was dead.

'You hear of out of body experiences. I felt like I was on the outside looking in on myself walking, running into the house,' he said.

'I went down to the bedroom and it was very bloody and very violent.

'Instinct just kicked in to try and revive her, do some sort of CPR, something and when I checked for a pulse or that, as Rose said she looked like marble, she felt like marble as well, very cold and very hard. I tried to move her but I couldn't. I don't know if that's because she was so stiff or because the life had drained out of me.'

And later as he watched the paramedics work on his wife, he said he knew there was nothing they could do.

'I knew if they brought Rachel back she was going to suffer massive brain damage and she'd never be the same again,' he said.

Joe referred once again to Rachel's sporting talents and how she was a strong woman who would have fought against her attackers.

'Certainly if this was, depending on what theory you're reading in the paper, if this was, two random burglars they certainly didn't break into the home of a defenceless little old lady.'

And Kenny, while not going so far as to ask Joe if he was a suspect, brought up the statistics that say eight to nine out of ten murder victims know their attacker. He then asked if Joe thought it was likely that Rachel's killer was someone she knew and trusted.

'Yes I think so,' Joe replied. 'Where the murder happened was in the bedroom which is the very last room in the house, so it's the room you're least likely to bring someone you don't know because you're cornered.

'It's not a police theory, it's just my own personal belief that she knew the person because why else would you kill her? If it's a violent robbery why go to the extreme of murdering the person unless they can identify you.

'There was a lot of blood and therefore there would have been a lot of blood on this person.'

Before finishing, Joe gave one final insight: 'Everyone, including myself, is a suspect until this is resolved,' he said firmly.

'I was questioned in the same way everyone else was and statistically, you know, it's usually the husband, boyfriend or whatever.

'If it's someone that we both know I will be shocked, probably physically sick too.'

Since the murder Joe had been staying at his mother's house, keeping his sons with him at all times. Once the examination of the murder scene was completed he was given back the keys to his house in Naul.

Joe then began to talk to the press in earnest.

Over and over again he went through the grisly events of the day Rachel was killed. He offered theories and showed journalists and photographers exactly where she had been beaten to death.

I was one of the reporters he spoke to.

CHAPTER 4

A Regular Joe

I HAD NO preconceptions about Joe before calling out to his home in Naul to interview him for the first time.

As far as I was concerned, I was calling out to a devastated widower and father of two small boys, who had no idea who killed his wife or why.

The only hint I was given that there could possibly have been more to this murder than met the eye was when I was advised by my news editor to ask Joe if he knew if he was being treated as a suspect.

It's not the kind of question that you like posing to a recently bereaved husband but it is a valid one given that a large proportion of murdered women are killed by their partners.

As it turned out Joe was more than happy to answer any questions that I asked him, no matter how awkward. From that first meeting, which lasted just under three hours, he seemed to be the ultimate people pleaser, a nice guy who liked people liking him.

And I did like him, I thought he was a really lovely man, who seemed to be in deep shock and although happy to give an interview, was conscious of how he would sound and kept apologising for using clichés to explain how the murder was affecting him.

In the weeks and months following the interview, when it emerged that Joe was indeed a major suspect for his wife's killing, I told anyone who cared to ask, and there were many, that I believed Joe was innocent.

Most people I have admitted that to since have either laughed in my face or gaped at me in utter astonishment and I suppose I can't really blame them.

But I realise now, with the benefit of hindsight of course, that during the ten months or so that I kept in contact with Joe, I wanted to believe this amiable and somewhat charismatic man was utterly incapable of beating his wife to death with a dumb-bell.

It was his geniality, I think, and his politeness that made it difficult for me to accept that Joe could have carried out such a horrific and meticulously planned murder.

Surely I would have noticed something about him that was weirdly different or even slightly creepy.

But Joe was so downright ordinary—so like a nice chatty fella you might work in the same office with, live beside, drink in the same pub as or be on the same sports team with.

And I don't think I would have so readily called to his home and spent hours talking to him about the brutal death of his wife, or met him at his office a couple of times to chat about how the investigation was going, if I really thought he was a murderer.

That was probably the most shocking thing about Joe, and one of the main reasons this case enthralled the nation. To the outside world he was totally normal.

But underneath this content and happy façade was a man who must have spent weeks if not months planning and working towards his wife's murder. And within moments of carrying out the brutal killing he threw himself into the role of the devastated widower, begging for people's help to catch whoever had bludgeoned Rachel to death.

And for a while, albeit briefly, he managed to fool a number of people—including me.

It was 21 October, a Thursday, when I was asked to call out to his home, less than three weeks after the murder.

It's routine in such circumstances for newspapers to enquire if the family of a murder victim might be willing to give an interview. Some people appreciate the chance to talk about who their loved one was, rather than have them just remembered as a victim of a hideous crime, while others hope it may help in some way with the murder investigation. And of course there are those who don't want, or feel unable, to talk at all.

Finding his home in Naul took some time. With the help of a colleague who had reported on the story the day after Rachel had been murdered and using Murphy's Quarry as a landmark, I finally came across the house.

The curtains were pulled and there was no answer at the front door. I decided to leave and head for Joe's mother's house; it had been reported that he was staying there with his two sons, Luke and Adam.

Ann O'Reilly lives in a relatively new housing estate in Dunleer in Co. Louth, also just off the M1. About a 20 minute drive further north from Beldarragh, it was much easier to locate.

There was no one there either, however, and so I made my way back to Beldarragh. This time Joe was home.

When he answered the front door his mother Ann was standing behind him. Both looked worn out. After sympathising with him on his loss and apologising for the intrusion, I explained why I was there and explained I hoped to interview him for an article that I was writing about Rachel.

In a friendly, though suitably downbeat manner, he nodded and replied that he was happy to talk to me but would not be free for another few hours. He asked me if I could come back later that evening. We settled on 8pm and when I asked him if it was okay to bring a photographer with me, he agreed.

We arrived a little early that night, about 10 or 15 minutes, but Joe greeted us warmly at the front door and ushered us into the kitchen.

It was chilly in the house, no doubt because he had not been living there since Rachel's death, and Joe was wearing a heavy woollen navy jumper with dark jeans.

Painted bright yellow, the large kitchen cum dining room was in a disheveled state with papers and documents strewn all over the table, for which Joe apologised before moving them out of the way.

It was an unremarkable room, obviously well lived in with children's drawings pinned to the wall beside the fridge, including a paper chick with 'Happy Mother's Day' written upon it. On the fridge door was a magnet that read 'Friends are the family we choose for ourselves.'

Joe is a big man, 6ft 5inches to be exact and well built with a slight paunch. Visibly nervous, which I have to say I found to be quite endearing, he fussed around for a while, making tea while chatting about the local area and how some people might find it quite isolated.

He had an easy manner and was instantly likeable. In fact when I realised I had forgotten to bring a notebook he immediately offered to dig out a spare blank one he had somewhere, it was no trouble: 'I know how these things happen.'

Eventually he sat down at the head of the kitchen table and we were ready to start.

He proved to be extremely easy to interview, articulate and happy, if not eager, to answer any questions put to him, including one or two that were decidedly awkward.

Throughout our lengthy conversation he spoke of 'Rach' in the present tense, an understandable mistake, I believed at the time, given the recentness of her death.

Almost immediately he began to rapidly recount the day of the murder. Jumping from when he came home that day to how Rachel's best friend Jackie arrived and he told her 'I think she's gone' and 'we have to do something.'

At almost breakneck speed yet in a calm and chatty manner, he described some of the more gruesome aspects of the day, for instance how his wife's head had been stuck to the carpet with the enormous amount of blood that had seeped from her wounds.

And he recollected how when the team of paramedics arrived it reminded him of a 'scene straight out of Holby City,' the hospital-based television drama series.

He spoke of his mother-in-law, Rose, the one to first discover Rachel's body, and who told Joe how she thought her daughter had maybe fallen.

Joe then explained that when he arrived home that day he had noticed the kitchen table had been moved and the place was in a mess.

For a few minutes we talked about who possibly could have killed Rachel and why. Joe told how his and Rachel's families had spoken of little else since the day of her slaying.

'We firmly believe it was someone she knew,' he said. 'Anyone that met her would know she wasn't stupid. If she'd stumbled across a burglary, she would have been straight out the door. She was very smart and not naive, there's no way she'd have risked her life staying in the house. Besides, there's a set of very sharp knives in our kitchen. Why didn't she take one of those to defend herself?

'She was killed in the bedroom, the last room in the house. She was trapped there with no way out. She wouldn't have let that happen unless she knew who the person was in the house with her.

'The gardaí asked me if I knew of anyone who might have had a grudge against her or me, but anyone who might have a problem with me wouldn't have known where we lived. And the type of person that Rachel was, well she just didn't hold grudges, she was straight, almost too straight and always cleared the air with people.'

An obvious question to ask at this point was might she have been having an affair?

'I quite honestly can say that I don't have any suspicions about that,' he said firmly.

'I've been going through all her stuff over the past number of days and I haven't found anything that would even hint she was seeing another man.

'Besides, the biggest thing about Rach was her straightness. She was almost too straight at times. If she had met someone else, she was far too honest and brave not to have told me. She would have said something immediately; that was the kind of person she was.'

A couple of seconds later, he added: 'Even if she was, what can I do about that now?'

All of which inevitably led to the next awkward question, did he realise that he was probably a suspect himself? And far from being angry or upset at the suggestion, Joe gladly spoke about how he had been warned by pals that people may start to point the finger at him.

'I had no idea about the statistics that say it's usually a spouse or partner who is the killer,' he said. 'It was actually friends of mine from work who told me and to say I was shocked is an understatement.

'It's funny but Rach would have definitely known something like that. She's really into TV crime shows and stuff like that. I didn't even realise the guards were treating it as a murder investigation until they told me.'

He revealed the first chat he had with the gardaí about his wife's murder.

'The night of the day she was killed I brought Luke and Adam to stay in my mother's house in Dunleer,' he explained.

'Three guards called round and said they had some questions for me. They started off by asking if I'd noticed anything missing, but then it was: "Did you ever hit her?" I couldn't believe it and they just explained it by saying, "You do know this is a murder investigation?"'

'I was too shocked to be angry and, besides, I knew in the back of my mind that they were doing their job; those kind of questions had to be asked.'

The conversation turned to their early life together and when they first met.

'She was 17 and I was about 19. I'd noticed her straight away because she's so tall, 5ft 11in,' Joe said with a smile. 'I'm 6ft 5in myself.'

He told how their relationship progressed after their first date at the cinema.

'At first, it was a kind of teenager thing. I remember she wouldn't introduce me to her family for ages because she wanted to make sure it was serious enough.

'Then, a couple of years later, I went to the States for a three-week summer holiday. I missed her so badly that I knew I wanted it to be more serious. But it wasn't until she went to Australia for a month that Christmas and realised she felt the same way that we decided to do something about it.

'We started saving money for our future; Rachel's very practical that way. Two years later, I proposed in Paris during the spring of 1994 on top of the Eiffel Tower.'

And he told how Rachel picked out her own engagement ring. 'I didn't have much choice about that one,' he smiled ruefully. 'She knew exactly what she wanted.'

It took a while, however, for the couple to move in together.

'Rach was very old-fashioned about stuff like that,' Joe explained.

'It was sweet, really. She wanted to do everything the right way round. We were engaged for about two years before we moved into our first house out in Santry. About a year later, we got married.'

He spoke fondly of their honeymoon in Kenya.

'We were supposed to go on two Safaris but I got sick and couldn't go on the second one,' Joe said.

'She was a real sun person but she said she'd stay with me and take care of me. But I told her to get down to the beach, there was no point the pair of us sitting indoors.'

It was around this point that Joe brought out their beautifully mounted, black leather wedding album. Laid out on the kitchen table, we bent over photographs showing the handsome couple exchanging vows.

This was also the first and only time during our chat that Joe showed any kind of real emotion. His eyes welling up with tears, he fell silent as the pages were turned and pictures of him with his arms wrapped around his wife stared back at us.

'I haven't seen a lot of these photos in a long time,' he said eventually.

The interview continued with Joe telling me about Rachel's difficult pregnancies.

'Being pregnant with Luke was bad but when she was pregnant with Adam it was even worse,' he said. 'She had to spend a lot of time in hospital and we decided then that the two boys were enough, or that we'd wait until they were both in school. That sort of thing runs you down.'

He also recalled her excitement at finding their 'dream home'.

'When we bought it, there was a lot of work that needed to be done but we were getting to it by degrees,' he said.

'Rach was brilliant when it came to household stuff. She put in the kitchen presses herself, hung the doors and even lay some of the wooden floors. Just during the last August bank holiday weekend, she built the decking that's out in the back garden.'

At one stage Joe proudly brought out the Guinness Book of World records certificate they received after participating in the longest continuous game of softball in the world.

'We did it at the very beginning of last May,' he beamed.

'We played for 55 hours and 11 minutes at St Mary's Rugby Club in Templeogue.'

Joe then returned to his version of events on the day of the murder.

'That morning, I'd gone to the gym as normal,' he began.

'I work in the Bluebell Industrial Estate on the Naas Road and have to be there by 8.30am. A while ago, Rachel suggested I join a gym, leave the house earlier in the morning and get a workout done instead of sitting in heavy traffic.

'She may also have hinted that I was getting fat,' he added, smiling.

'Adam, my younger boy, goes to a Montessori school in Naul and finishes there at 12.30pm. At 1.15pm, I got a call from the lady who runs the school to say that Rach hadn't picked him up yet. Obviously she'd rung Rach a few times but she couldn't get through.

'I immediately called Rach's mobile but it rang through to the message minder and then I tried the house but there was no answer.

'Jackie is Rach's best friend and it was her birthday that day so I thought maybe she was at her house so I rang her but she was still in bed. She's a nurse and was on nights. All this time, I just thought there must have been some kind of mix-up. A lot of the mums from around the area would sometimes take it in turns to pick up the kids.

'I then rang Rose Callaly, Rach's mum, and when she said she hadn't seen her I began to get a sick feeling in my stomach. I left work and went to pick up Adam. All sorts of things were going through my head: "Maybe she'd gone for a swim and her mobile was in a locker."

'I got a call from Rach's dad, asking for some of our neighbours' phone numbers. He thought that she could have fallen while doing some DIY.

'In the meantime, Rach's mum—perhaps it was a mother's intuition—had driven straight to our house. After picking up Adam, I went to Luke's school to see where he was. He'd been picked up already and I felt such relief, thinking it was Rach who'd collected him. But it turned out it was one of our neighbours.

'I then headed home and I saw that her car was still parked outside. As I made my way into the house, Rach's mum came towards me. Her face was so white I knew something had happened.

'I asked her what was wrong and she just said, "I think she's dead." Rach's friend and our neighbour, Sarah, were in the kitchen. She was bawling crying and trying to ring the emergency services. I ran past her down the hall and into the bedroom.

'Rach was lying there on the floor and there was so much blood. I tried CPR on her, thinking I could revive her, but as soon as I touched her I knew something was seriously wrong. She was as cold as marble. And the damage that had been done to her head? To be honest, I don't think I'll ever be able to talk about it properly.'

It was at this point that Joe suddenly asked us if we would like to see where it had happened. Taken aback I looked at my colleague in confusion and then asked Joe if he meant the bedroom where Rachel had been killed.

'Yeah, it's a bit of a mess because of the work the forensics people had to do but you can see where we found her,' he replied.

Although distinctly uneasy I found myself following Joe down the corridor of the bungalow to the main bedroom. Uncomfortable with the idea of actually entering the bedroom, the photographer and I looked in from the hallway. As it was, we had a perfect view of the spot where Rachel's body had been found.

The carpet on which she had been found sprawled had been cut and taken away. Although not quite the chalk outline familiar from American cop shows, the effect was similar.

We stood there for several minutes in silence.

The room was decidedly untidy. There were no sheets or covers on the double bed, just a couple of plastic bags that appeared to be filled with clothes.

Joe then began to point out some details we may have missed—for instance the blood splatters on the walls: 'There and there, and that's more blood there,' he told us. Even if you have no knowledge of forensics it was impossible not to guess that the attack on Rachel must have been extremely violent to cause blood to fly around the room like that.

He also explained that the door and entire doorframe to the bedroom had been taken away by the forensic team to be examined. 'We've all been talking about this non-stop,' he said. 'I'm not a pathologist, of course these are just my own opinions. But Rachel was 5ft 11ins and she was a strong woman, she used to be a shot putt thrower and we used to give play digs to each other sometimes and hers really hurt. If she had feared for her life she would have hit with everything she had.

'That guy would have been left with a mark, he would have been hurt.'

He was so calm and clinical about the whole thing that I wondered for a few minutes at the weirdness of it all. But then I reasoned that he was still in shock and this was his way of coping, or maybe he had become used to coming down here in the days since his wife had been killed.

Having never personally experienced the death of a loved one, let alone had a family member brutally murdered, I quickly decided I was in no position to question his demeanour or actions. After all, death affects different people in very different ways.

Feeling decidedly nauseous, I asked Joe if I could use his bathroom. 'Sure, second door on your left there behind you.'

Turning around I noticed the room directly behind me was the boys' bedroom and then made my way into the bathroom where I stayed for several minutes breathing deeply and waiting for the queasiness to pass.

When I came out Joe was back in the kitchen with the photographer. We resumed the interview and immediately I asked him what did he plan to do with the house?

It was surprising to hear that he eventually intended to move his family back in.

'It's a really lovely area and what's happened has happened. There are so many great people near-by and the schools are fantastic. Besides, it was Rach's place and everything about it has to do with her,' he explained.

'The boys are so young now that I'm afraid they'll forget everything they know about her—so, hopefully, living here will help them hold on to their memories. But if they're not happy here then of course we'll move on.'

And he spoke about a trunk of Rachel's things he was putting together so their children would have something substantial to remember their mother by.

'Jackie, Rachel's sister, and a few other close friends are going through her stuff and picking out the bits and pieces she loved best to put into the trunk,' he explained. 'They've also been putting little photo albums together, scrapbooks with loads of different memories and some video footage that we have, so her life will be there in words and pictures.'

'It's funny: going through some presses in the house I found a lighter and an empty box of cigarettes. I'd no idea she was a smoker. As far as I know it was the only secret she ever kept from me. And it looks like I was the only one who didn't know; when I mentioned it to my mother and Jackie they both said they knew.'

But then the mood darkened again as he told of how hard it had been trying to explain to his son Luke that his mummy was gone away for good.

'Rachel's aunt Lucy died last year and Rachel told him that she had gone to play with the stars,' Joe said.

'So that's what I told Luke but he just looked at me and said: "No, mummy's coming home."

'And we both just started to bawl crying. He held on to me until he finally fell asleep. It was as though he was afraid that I was going to leave as well. Since then, he keeps asking questions, all the time. He's absorbed a lot of information for a four-year-old and of course he's heard things at school from the other kids.'

Joe said his other son, Adam, was too young to understand and he dreaded having to sit them both down when they were older to tell them that Rachel had been murdered.

'I'll have to tell them of course,' he said. 'But it's something I'm going to have to talk through with counsellors first and see what the best way to approach it will be.

'Friends are keeping all the newspaper clippings for me. I haven't been able to look at any of them yet, but in years to come they'll be there for me to show the boys.'

Once again the conversation turned to who the killer might be.

'Well I know the police are all over this investigation,' Joe said with a firm nod of his head.

'No stone has been left unturned. And you know even if it was a random burglar, I bet they got the shock of their lives when they came across Rachel. She wasn't some weak, little old lady.'

Joe then agreed to pose for some photos for us. We had noticed that during the interview he had been constantly toying with a narrow gold band on the little finger of his left hand. It was Rachel's, he told us, a ring she had never taken off since the day they were married and it was one of the few pieces of her jewellery he had left.

Although claiming to be uncomfortable having his photo taken, he posed easily and happily raised his hand to his face so we could get a shot of the wedding band.

As the camera flashed, Joe continued to chat about how he had been coping since his wife's death. 'It's the little things so far,' he sighed. 'I know it's a cliché but it really is just one day at a time. There are so many memories and everything I do even now she had always been involved in.

'But you know it's not just me and the kids who've been affected by her death. There are the two families of course and she had a huge circle of friends, not to mention all the softball people. God there must be about 1,000 people touched by this.'

The photographs taken, Joe then gathered a selection of his own photographs of Rachel, himself and their two little boys as well as their wedding album that he allowed us to borrow and scan later in the office.

Even as we prepared to leave he still volunteered information.

'She was very honest,' he said. 'Very loyal and we had a very honest relationship. If we had something to say we said it. That's why I think if she had been having a relationship she'd have been brave and honest enough to tell me.'

Walking us to the front door he warmly, not to mention firmly, shook both our hands. As we thanked him for his time he said not to mention it, all he asked of us was that we did 'Rach proud.'

Driving back to the M1, we sat in silence for several mintues, aborbing all that we had just heard and witnessed.

'Jesus, that was seriously intense,' I said to my colleague. Half jokingly I asked: 'Do you think there's any chance that he could have done it?'

'I don't know,' he replied cautiously. 'I just don't know. I really hope not; he seems like a really nice guy.'

'Well, I don't think he did it,' and for the next few months that was the answer I gave to anyone who asked me about meeting Joe. Yet looking back on my notes from that night, there was obviously something niggling at the back of my mind.

'No talk of how much he loved her, never said he'll miss her,' I wrote. And one of his quotes had bothered me enough that I had highlighted it.

'She was straight, almost too straight, always said what she thought.'

And over the next couple of years I went over those notes several times, looking for anything else that might have struck me as odd that night.

But all I could see was that I had come away thinking what a normal, nice guy he had seemed to be. A regular Joe.

CHAPTER 5

Not So Mr Nice Guy

TOWARDS THE VERY end of that October, I phoned Joe to arrange the return of his wedding album. Although polite and friendly, there was no mistaking the stress in his voice. So I asked him how things were going.

'I'm not doing too good,' he replied.

A couple of nights prior to that, RTE had broadcast a reconstruction of Rachel's movements on the day she was murdered.

'That Crimecall programme was really hard to watch but I thought they did it really well.

'For some reason the whole thing really hit me yesterday, it was my son's birthday and reading all the birthday cards and Rachel not being here, well I've been a basket case ever since to tell you the truth.'

He complained about some of the newspaper coverage.

'Yours was the most decent piece in any of the papers,' he said. 'Thank you and I really mean it, you did her proud. But I'm just glad the whole media thing is over now.'

The 'media thing' was far from over. He was forced to deny rumours that were circulating about his relationship with another woman at the time of Rachel's death. 'There is no other woman in my life and I have never had an affair—absolutely and definitely not,' he told one newspaper. [1]

Strong words indeed from a man who had already admitted to gardaí that he had been seeing his former work colleague, although he had certainly played down the affair and claimed it had been over at the time of Rachel's death.

Yet despite his well-founded fears that revelations of his affair might arouse even further suspicion, it didn't prevent him from appearing in public with his lover in the weeks after Rachel's death.

Naomi Gargan, whose children went to the same school as the O'Reilly boys, would later reveal how Joe introduced her to a woman at his son Adam's birthday party at the Leisureplex in Coolock on 24 October. She had blonde hair and her name was Nikki.

Nikki Pelley is an attractive, slim and confident thirty-something.

'Nikki was stunning,' said one former colleague from her days at Xtravision in the late 1980s. 'She was fit, blonde, spoke beautifully, comes from a really good family, a real southsider. [2]

'She was an area manager for the company, which meant she had to wear this striking black and red uniform and drive one of the black and red jeeps you used to see flying around the place.

'It was all very glamorous at the time and on top of that Nikki was a really good worker, very efficient and smart.'

Joe first met Nikki in 2002 while both of them were working at Viacom. Nikki was based at the head office in Fitzwilliam Square and Joe at the Bluebell Industrial Estate, but they got to know each other through general work meetings and staff nights.

Their physical relationship, however, did not start until mid-2004. By this stage Nikki had moved to Maiden Outdoor Advertising, a subsidiary of Viacom based in Dundrum; it was much nearer to her home in Rathfarnham.

In January 2004, she arranged to meet some of her old work colleagues in the Barge Pub on the Grand Canal in Dublin. Joe was there that evening and the two fell into easy conversation and swapped email addresses before the night was over.

They began to regularly swap jokes and funny stories by email. This soon graduated to meeting for lunch a few weeks later at the Templeogue Inn in south Dublin and after that they went to the cinema together at The Liffey Valley shopping centre. Within four months of meeting that first night, they had begun to have a sexual affair and Joe was staying over at Nikki's place, an annexe off her parents' home in Rathfarnham, every Tuesday night.

As the affair grew more intense, Joe began to sleep over every Saturday night at Nikki's and introduced her to his two sons. The four would spend Saturday afternoons together at favourite family locations like the zoo.

✤ ✤ ✤ ✤ ✤

For a short time the media frenzy around the case had died down.

But on 16 November 2004, Nikki and Quearney were both suddenly arrested for questioning.

Quearney, a 44-year-old former member of the Defence Forces, was arrested in Ballyfermot at 10am and brought to Drogheda Garda station in Louth.

Nikki, then 36, was arrested an hour later in Dundrum and taken to Balbriggan Garda Station in north Dublin.

They were both held under Section 30 of the Offences Against the State Act, which allowed the officers to hold them without charge for up to 72 hours.

The two were not considered to be suspects but were arrested as a matter of routine in relation to the over-all investigation. They were now being questioned on suspicion of withholding information during previous interviews by the gardaí.

But Nikki and Quearney's arrests were completely overshadowed when Joe was picked up by the gardaí the following day at his home in Naul, just after 10am.

He was brought to the Drogheda station and held for questioning under Section 4 of the Criminal Justice Act for almost 12 hours. That afternoon, pictures of him being led away from his house appeared on the front page of *The Evening Herald*.

Thanks to the publicity a crowd began to gather at the police station from about 7pm, and by the time Joe was released without charge later that night he was greeted by the curious stares of the fifty or so locals who were waiting outside.

Dozens of photographers and journalists shouted questions and thrust cameras into his face, but for once refusing to comment, Joe walked quickly to a car being driven by his brother. It took several minutes for the car to start but once in gear, it sped off, Joe looking grim-faced and without a backward glance.

That same evening Quearney and Pelley were also both released without charge.

A few days later, I was asked to call out to Joe to see if he was interested in doing another interview. He was not at the house in Beldarragh, so I called up to his mother's home in Dunleer.

She answered the door and although reluctant to say too much, she was extremely polite and said she was refusing to read the newspapers anymore. Her other son Derek O'Reilly also came to the door.

Extraordinarily like his younger brother, except shorter, he was also polite yet understandably wary. He spoke about the 'rubbish and lies' the newspapers were reporting and said the only paper worth reading was the one Eamonn Dunphy wrote for, which was *Ireland on Sunday*. Dunphy had recently written a column arguing that it was not the media's job to convict a man of a crime he had not been found guilty of.

After I explained that I was from the same paper they thawed a little and we chatted for twenty minutes or so at the front door, throughout which I was conscious I could hear the unmistakable sounds of an adult man playing with children coming from upstairs.

Ann and Derek were clearly angry at how Joe was being treated by the Garda Síochána.

'As far as I can see they haven't even looked into the possibility it was someone else,' she said. 'It's like they decided from the very beginning it was Joe and they've been trying to pin it on him ever since.'

She and Derek then claimed that Joe had been encouraged to give media interviews by the gardaí.

I asked Ann if Joe was around and if she thought he'd be interested in talking to me. She insisted he wasn't at her house but before I left she told me Joe was 'being thrown to the wolves' by the gardaí.

'He did everything they told him to,' she said.

'He gave interviews to the newspapers even though he didn't want to. He was told it could help to catch Rachel's killer. We've been told since that the gardaí always brief you before you talk to the media. Nothing like that happened for Joe; they sent him in blind.'

And she reminded me of the two boys who had lost their mother.

'We had to take Adam and Luke out of school. We hate the idea of the disruption but what can we do?' she asked, genuinely distressed. 'They know something is going on but most of the time they're just confused little boys. It's heartbreaking to see.'

❖ ❖ ❖ ❖ ❖

By the beginning of December Joe had kept to his word and moved back into the house in Naul with his two sons. Still on compassionate leave from his job, he appeared to be trying to make life as normal as possible for the youngsters and was seen dropping them to school.

In the meantime, gardaí were convinced they were close to a major breakthrough in the murder case.

Ever since Rachel's body had been discovered, up to 35 detectives from the National Bureau of Criminal Investigation (NBCI) and local garda officers had been holding daily conferences and working together to gather as much evidence and information as possible.

More than 700 witness statements were taken, making it one of the biggest murder investigations in years.

Soon there were whispers of a vital piece of evidence that gardaí believed placed Joe near the murder scene the morning of 4 October rather than at the Broadstone depot, as he had claimed in his statement.

Just a few days after Joe's release from Drogheda Garda Station it was revealed that this 'vital evidence' was his mobile phone records. The 'cell site' analysis of phone calls and texts made and received on his phone that day showed it had been in the vicinity of his house in Naul around the time of Rachel's death.

It was also reported that Gardaí were now concentrating on the CCTV footage that they believed showed a car like Joe's close to his home at the time of Rachel's murder.

It helped that Joe's car was not a very common model found on Irish roads. A Ford Marea, it is a distinctive, large estate car, and officers spent weeks tracking down as many other owners of the same model as they could find in an effort to eliminate them from the CCTV footage.

Despite the evidence piling up against him, Joe's family were sticking firmly by his side.

'If I thought for a second that Joe had anything to do with Rachel's death I would disown him,' Ann O'Reilly told one reporter. [3]

'He is a good and kind-natured son and it is not in his character to be violent to anyone, he would not be allowed under my roof.

'Anyone who knows Joe and the relationship he had with Rachel would know he positively had no involvement in her murder. People will say I am his mother and naturally I would stand by him, that is what mothers do. But no-one knows Joe better than me. I reared him and brought him up and I know what I am talking about.

'As far as I am concerned he has been in a state of shock since day one.'

And although the press continued to speculate and the gardaí continued to investigate, there was little evidence to show they were closer to charging anyone with Rachel's murder.

In March 2006 the then Minister for Justice, Michael McDowell, gave gardaí permission to exhume Rachel's remains. Orders for exhumations are rare, though they are granted in exceptional circumstances and news of this latest move in the on-going investigation was naturally seen as being of massive significance.

Beginning work at the graveside at 6.30am on 8 March, members of the Garda Technical Bureau carried out a forensic examination for about two hours before returning Rachel's remains into the grave.

The following day it was reported that the officers had discovered a series of notes and letters in the coffin and that one in particular had been brought back to the garda headquarters in the Phoenix Park to be examined. There were rumours that the letter or note was badly decomposed and that it was going to prove difficult to decipher.

But it was believed the contents of the letter would help lead investigating officers to the killer.

'It's not uncommon for family or friends to place letters and other items in a loved one's coffin before burial,' a senior garda officer was quoted at the time. [4]

'We're hopeful that this particular letter will significantly enhance this investigation.

'At first, the witness who tipped us off didn't attach any significance to the letter but we believe it could be crucial and will assess its impact later this week.'

On the same day that Rachel's body was exhumed, an inquest into her death ruled she had died after sustaining severe multiple head injuries, including a fractured skull and damage to her brain.

Dr Marie Cassidy, the State Pathologist, had told how a post mortem she carried out on Rachel's body revealed the cause of death to be blunt force trauma to the head, inhalation of blood, a fractured skull and scalp lacerations. She said there was also 'evidence of damage to the brain.'

✤ ✤ ✤ ✤ ✤

In mid-April I called up to the house in Naul once again to ask Joe if he knew of anything new happening in the investigation. It was a bright, sunny, spring day and the two O'Reilly boys were playing in the front garden. The garage door was open and as I got nearer I could see Joe getting his lawn mower ready to take out.

He looked up and immediately turned off the motor. Walking towards me he had a friendly, if resigned, look on his face and we shook hands.

'Look I know you have to call up,' he said after I apologised for disturbing him.

'You've been the most impartial of the newspapers, you've given both sides.'

We then talked about how things were going in general for him and his family.

'It's getting harder if truth be told,' he said.

'I see the two boys getting older and Rach is not here to see it. I went back to work and it's been fine, those people know me and it says something that they've been fine around me.'

He then spoke of how he seemed to be instantly recognisable, thanks to all the media coverage. 'People seem to know who I am,' he said.

'I get stared at a lot but I couldn't care less. There's a lot of stuff people don't know and I can't say anything yet, I'm under strict instructions from my solicitor but it's all in hand.'

We chatted a bit about the fine weather and a little about how the boys were getting on.

Throughout our informal chat I wondered about what it was, the 'stuff' people didn't know, but looking at his calm and friendly demeanour, it really did seem like it was all 'in hand.'

We spoke by phone a couple of more times, usually me just asking if there was any news from the investigation he felt he could talk about. The answer was always a firm no, but he was friendly and insisted he didn't mind my checking in.

Then on 25 April 2005 a Sunday newspaper reported that Joe's managerial job at Viacom was being merged with another position and he was being forced to re-apply if he wanted to stay working at the company.

I rang Joe again to see what was happening.

'I don't know where they got that stuff from,' he said.

He confirmed, however, that his job had been merged with another position and was told he would have to re-apply. 'I'll be taking it to the Labour Court,' he said. 'In fact I was promised a directorship but when I got back after my leave of absence it was gone.'

The next time I contacted Joe again was by text on the morning of 28 June. He replied promptly: 'Free from 3.30 until 5ish in Bluebell if you are around.'

I drove to the Viacom offices off the Long Mile Road in south Dublin that afternoon. Joe seemed to be in the offices on his own but as he led me into a small conference room he shouted in the direction of a warehouse out the back: 'Watch the phones will ya?'

Wearing a striped light-coloured shirt, he looked as though he had put on some weight. His hair was tightly cropped and very black and I remember wondering if he had dyed it.

After offering me coffee or water, Joe sat down with me at the table and was as affable and chatty as ever.

Joe was obviously in a chatty mood. The conversation moved on to the Callalys and the stories that had appeared in various papers that claimed Rachel's family had not seen Luke and Adam in weeks, if not months.

'I've never once said they can't see the boys,' he insisted. 'In fact I want them to see the boys.'

He then spoke of a row that had broken out over Rachel's headstone and his rather unpleasant attitude towards the devastated Callalys was uncomfortable to listen to.

'Luke, my little 5-year-old picked one out,' he claimed. 'It's really tasteful, in fact the guy who made it wants to use a photo of it for his catalogue. But it turns out the plot for Rachel's grave is in her father's name.'

As a result, Joe claimed, he was being stopped from putting up the headstone by the Callaly family. At that point, he began to tell lies about his in-laws.

'God knows why,' Joe said, rolling his eyes dramatically. 'It doesn't say anything like "forgive me," or "I killed her."'

'And I'd just like to point out,' he went on. 'No one in her family has been near her grave for weeks. I'm the only one who goes up there.'

His rant and lies about the Callalys did not end there. 'All this stuff about the Callalys being so close to Rachel and the boys is not true,' he said. 'Rachel had a row with her mother two weeks before she died. There was always a lot of tension because Rach made a lot more effort with her parents than they did with her. It led to a lot of rows.'

This was all lies but he continued to vent his anger and continued to lie.

'Rachel would get upset that her parents never visited her or the boys in Naul. Adam only stayed over once in his grandparents' house, Luke never stayed there, ever.

'The day after Rachel was killed the boys were in their grandparents' house. They were grieving badly yet they weren't allowed into the kitchen, they were only allowed stay in the sitting room in case they messed things up. What does that tell you?'

And still he was not finished his tirade against the shattered family of his murdered wife.

'I want them [his sons] to see their grandparents,' he said. 'They rang my mother at one stage and arranged to pick them up on a Friday but they never arrived and I haven't seen or heard from them since, that was five weeks ago. Doting grandparents? I don't think so.'

This was a side that few people had seen. The claims were made up in his head because Rachel's family were pushing for justice.

Calming down a little he began to shake his head. 'You know they let Rach down a lot,' he said. 'They're not the loving, close family they claim to be.'

It was a lengthy outpouring against his wife's family but his allegations rang false. The Callalys' grief in the aftermath of the murder had been all too real. I had called up to their home the same day I met Joe. Rachel's father Jimmy answered the door and brought me inside to the kitchen. It was clear to see he was a broken man, almost incapacitated with pain and I left quickly, realising he was in no fit state to talk to anyone about his daughter's death.

For the first time, Joe had let his amiable, friendly façade slip and behind it was a disturbing and distasteful side to his character.

He told me how he had a list of things he had to sort out; number one was clearing his name, two was finding Rachel's killers, the third was suing the guards followed by suing the newspapers, and the fifth was going to the Labour Court over losing out the directorship of the company.

We also talked about his work colleague, Derek Quearney.

'He's not a good friend of mine or anything like that,' claimed Joe.

'In fact the first thing I did when I got this job was fire one of his pals. I also got a job he probably felt was his, he had no reason whatsoever to cover for me.

'It was really embarrassing going back into work and having to face him; all I could do was say sorry.'

Our chat finished up and Joe walked me to the door before shaking my hand. Two weeks later I had to return to his offices again.

A daily newspaper had run yet another front-page story about the investigation into Rachel's murder, catapulting it into the headlines again. In the meantime, my paper had heard of the row about Rachel's headstone during routine enquires and was running a story about it.

I thought I should let Joe know.

He greeted me at the door of the Bluebell offices and led me into the same little meeting room. We chatted briefly about the hot weather and the bad traffic; it was all very friendly. But then I told him about the story planned for that Sunday. His demeanour changed immediately. He sat back in his chair and said nothing. I assured him that I was not going to divulge anything he had told me in our previous conversations, but he just stared at me stonily and I thought it best to shut up and stare back.

Eventually he asked me what was going to be in the story. I outlined the gist of what I knew and told him they had got it from another source. He didn't appear to believe me.

It was, to say the least, a tense 20 minutes.

Eventually he asked if the story was going to be on the front page. When I said it probably wouldn't, he relaxed a little and explained that he didn't want the boys to see it.

The conversation lightened a little and he told me that other friends had been brought in for questioning again; they had been asked if they had talked to newspapers.

But despite him being friendly again and saying he appreciated me coming out to tell him about the upcoming story, I was slightly shaken by his reaction. And maybe he sensed that because as I walked to the door he cracked a joke about how I must have 'feared' for my life.

Without thinking I answered that yes, I had been pretty nervous.

For a split second he looked genuinely hurt. I tried to recover by joking that he'd probably start sending me expletive texts once he read the story. He quickly replied that wasn't his style.

That was the last contact I had with Joe.

Over the next fifteen months as the gardaí continued with their investigation, Joe occupied himself with bringing up his two boys. Stories about the murder case appeared in the press every so often, and while it was certainly not forgotten, there were few new revelations to report.

But behind the scenes the Gardaí were pulling together all the information they had painstakingly been gathering.

In March 2006 Joe and his girlfriend Nikki were arrested once again and taken to the garda station in Drogheda in Co. Louth. Nikki's second arrest was once again a matter of routine; she was not suspected of any crime. It's believed the two were questioned about 18 phone calls and texts they had sent each other on the day of the murder.

Again both were released without charge but if either of them thought interest in their arrests would quickly die down, they were mistaken.

As Nikki's mother Margaret was collecting her from the garda station, her father Fraser decided to ring *Liveline*, the afternoon show on RTE Radio One.

But instead of alleviating the situation, it probably increased media interest.

'There was a relationship between Nikki and Joe before Rachel was murdered,' he said.

'She [Nikki] 100 per cent believes Joe is innocent. Nothing has altered her mind since November 2004 to today.'

He went on to explain to the show's presenter Joe Duffy and his substantial live radio audience that the attention Nikki's arrest had attracted had been very difficult for him and his family.

He also described how Nikki had been arrested, that she had called him two days earlier to say that a car was following her and she thought it was a newspaper photographer but in fact it had been the gardaí. And when she had pulled into her home and got out of her car, an officer told her she was being arrested.

Pelley, however, had no doubts that his daughter would be fine, that she had dealt with being arrested before.

'She coped with it very well, she has nothing to hide. We know her—she had nothing to hide.'

The gardaí had also spoken to him about their relationship with Joe.

'Myself and my wife were interviewed yesterday for about an hour,' he said. 'They were very nice the two of them. Basically they just wanted to get our opinion of what we thought about Joe and the family.'

'We told them the truth. We've known him now for nearly 18 months, we know his children very well and he is very good with them. We have seen nothing that would indicate that he was involved in the murder but that's just our opinion.'

By June 2006 the investigating team were confident enough with their results to send a file to the Director of Public Prosecutions. It was the DPP who would decide whether there was enough evidence to finally charge Joe with the murder of his wife Rachel.

✤ ✤ ✤ ✤ ✤

On the second anniversary of Rachel's death, her family held a prayer vigil outside the house where she had been killed. More than 200 people turned up outside the bungalow in Naul. Joe, who was still living in the house at the time, was nowhere to be seen.

Rachel's sister, Anne, spoke to the gathered friends and relatives, telling them she wanted people to know her sister as a person and not just a victim.

'She was not just a name in a newspaper,' Anne told them. 'She was vivacious and larger than life. She was a beautiful daughter to her heartbroken mam and dad and a great sister to us.

'She was like a gust of wind; her presence filled everywhere she went. She was outgoing and sporty and she had no fear. She was never shy and was the life and soul of the party. She had a charisma that grew with her into adulthood.

'She was great at everything,' Anne continued. 'And she did love a challenge and succeeded nine times out of ten. Her heart was full of generosity and goodwill, she would do anything for you that she could. Her energy was amazing.'

Anne then spoke to her dead sister: 'Yours is a life that cannot be replaced, a void that cannot be filled,' she said. 'Rachel we know you are with us, stay near. You are always loved and never forgotten.'

Rose told the vigil how her family wanted Rachel to know she was not alone.

'Rachel had such a lonely parting,' she said 'We felt last year it was still very, very raw but this year we felt we just wanted to let her know that everybody is still thinking about her and everybody cares. We feel everybody is behind her, but what we want now is justice, of course we want justice for her, that's the big thing.'

The family stood in an intimate circle; the rest of those there to pray stood at a respectful distance but close enough to hear what was being said.

Rachel's eldest brother Declan read out the prayers of the faithful during ceremony while her sister-in-law, Denise and her aunt Susan Woods gave readings. And while Rachel's love of her sons, Luke and Adam was spoken of several times, there was no mention of Joe.

A framed photograph was placed at the gate into the house; it showed Rachel beaming with her arms wrapped around her sons. And her mother Rose, in honour of Rachel's love of singing, gave a rendition of the Irish folk song, *My Son*, with the lyrics slightly changed to suit the occasion.

'Rachel you were the gift of life to me and now you can no longer be.

'With pride we watched you grow up, you wanted so much to change the world for me.

'Rach, you gave our simple life its key.

'But Rach you faced the truth and you stood tall, and now we face the hardest truth of all.

'For you had to say goodbye, and we must go on living.

'But when our life is through, we will always be with
you, together with your song.'

It was an emotional service that left most people in
tears. And the knowledge that two years later, Rachel's
killer had still not been brought to justice must have
been difficult to bear.

This was something her family admitted when
Rose and Anne once again appeared on the *Late Late
Show* just two days after the vigil. It was one of the few
times any of the Callalys spoke about their loss and if
anyone was under any illusion that life had got easier
for the family in the years since Rachel's body had
been found, they soon knew better.

'At the time, you don't think of the length of time it
would take,' Rose explained.

'I certainly wouldn't have thought two years on,
there wouldn't have been anyone brought to justice.
This time two years ago, you are thinking in terms of
time, you are living day by day.

'It's extremely difficult because you might see a
headline that would startle you. You are just living
for the phone to ring, living in hope that there will
be justice. It is not enough to keep Rachel's memory
alive—we need justice for her too.'

She appealed once again for anyone with any
knowledge at all about the murder to come forward.
'The guilt still hangs over us,' she explained.

'Even though there is nothing we could have done,
you can't help but feel guilty.'

Her daughter, Anne, then tried to put into words the utter devastation she and the rest of her family had been experiencing since Rachel's murder.

'Sometimes I just don't enjoy anything anymore,' she said simply.

'You wake up and think is it ever going to get any better? Other times you forget that your family has been torn apart and wake up thinking she's alive. You just try to be normal but it seems like time stands still. I don't even know what day it is sometimes.'

Less than two weeks later, on 19 October 2006, the DPP finally gave the gardaí permission to charge Joe with murder. His trial was set for the following June.

The next time I saw Joe he was sitting alone on a bench in the Round Hall of the Four Courts, reading a newspaper as he waited for the courtroom to open.

Across from him was the Callaly family, who could barely bring themselves to look in his direction. It was a curious scene, to see Joe looking so nonchalant, casually turning the pages of his paper when you knew that shortly he would be asked how he pleaded to the charge of killing his wife.

The inscrutable, blank look on his face became a familiar sight to everyone who attended the trial over the next 21 days. It was a guise that slipped rarely during the four weeks of evidence that was set to shock, repulse and captivate the nation.

CHAPTER 6

The State Vs Joe O'Reilly

AT APPROXIMATELY 12.15PM on 25 June 2007, Joseph Anthony O'Reilly walked into Court No 2 of the Four Courts to stand trial for the murder of his wife.

He paused briefly at the back of the courtroom to get his bearings, towering over those standing around him. Politely excusing himself, he made his way through the large crowd, which had fallen silent as soon as he had appeared, and clutching a black leather folder and notebook, he took his seat.

Studiously ignoring the stares of those present in the crammed courtroom, he busied himself looking through notes and spent several minutes trying to get his large frame into a comfortable position on the narrow, straight-backed wooden bench.

The tense atmosphere in the room was conspicuous. Already the trial was starting a week late because the judge assigned to the case, Justice Barry White, had been busy with other court business and unable to start on the original trial date. But this time it looked as though the hearing was ready to finally begin.

Family, friends, gardaí, witnesses, journalists and onlookers had been arriving since before 10am, conscious that this was the most high-profile murder trial to happen in recent years and that seating space in the courtroom was limited.

The Callaly family, Jimmy, Rose, Declan, Paul, Anne and Anthony, sat side by side on a bench reserved for them.

They silently filed into the Central Criminal Court just before 11am and the courtroom, already packed, respectfully fell quiet as the family settled in. The strain and exhaustion on each of their faces was plain to see and there was little conversation between them, apart from the odd whisper, as they waited for the hearing to begin.

Sitting just a few metres away was Rachel's birth family, the Lowes.

Theresa was accompanied by her children and two of her sisters, who were also dressed in black. With their blonde hair and broad features, the resemblance between Rachel and her birth family was startling. On her own, sitting three benches behind the Lowes, talking to no one and staring straight ahead, was Joe's mother Ann.

Just before 12.30pm, the court rose as the trial judge took his seat.

And once the jury was brought in it was time to start. Acting on behalf of the State was Denis Vaughan-Buckley, a senior counsel who has worked on some of the biggest murder trials of the last decade. Almost immediately he admitted to the jury that the prosecution's case was wholly reliant on circumstantial evidence.

'Whilst this case is almost totally based on circumstantial evidence, I would submit to you that when you have heard everything you will be more than satisfied there is ample evidence that the accused did murder his wife,' the barrister began.

'You will be satisfied he did have a motive. You will be satisfied he also had the opportunity to commit the crime.

'There is no issue that Rachel O'Reilly was murdered,' he added.

'Whether or not she was murdered by her husband Joe, that is the issue.'

And in the rest of his forty minute or so opening statement, he told how 'you'd be less than human if you didn't have sympathy for Joe O'Reilly who is accused of murder. And likewise you'd be less than human if you didn't feel sympathy for the family and friends of Rachel, her brothers and sisters and her parents.'

For the benefit of the jury, the barrister turned and pointed out exactly where Rachel's parents, Jimmy and Rose were sitting.

Expressionless, the elderly couple stared back at the nine men and three women.

As he continued with his statement, going through some of the witnesses he planned to call and the evidence the jury could expect to hear, Joe listened intently, bending his head at times to take notes on his A4 notepad.

For the most part, the courtroom listened in taut silence, at times straining to hear everything the barrister said.

But when it came to describing the gruesome injuries Rachel had sustained, it proved too much for members of her family.

As the court heard the specific details of how Rachel's skull had been fractured during the attack causing severe injuries to her brain, her younger sister Anne quietly broke down in tears.

Her head bowed and hair obscuring her face, her shoulders shook uncontrollably as she sobbed. Her brother Anthony quickly put his arm around her.

But it was the letter written by Joe and found with her body when it was exhumed that caused most interest. For the moment, the barrister read just one small, carefully chosen, portion.

'This is the hardest letter I have had to write for reasons only we know. Rachel, forgive me.'

The barrister assured the jurors that there were 'more than ample enough witnesses' to help them 'safely come to the conclusion that the accused did kill his wife on 24th October 2004.'

He revealed one of these witnesses would be Rachel's friend, Helen Reddy. And that she would tell them how Joe had spoken to her on the evening of Rachel's murder and told her that no sexual assault had occurred and the police had confirmed this.

'How did the accused know no sexual assault before the post mortem?' he asked.

'He might have known if he was the one who killed his wife.'

The defence team was led by Patrick Gageby, a respected senior counsel. He reminded the court that this was a 'case enormously about facts'.

Also on that first day, the trial dramatically faced its first threat of collapse. Just after lunch, the judge told the court that it had been brought to his attention that one of the female jury members had a conversation about the case with a member of the jury panel shortly before she was sworn in. In this conversation, she told how she had heard rumours about the Joe O'Reilly case at her work-place.

There was an audible groan in the courtroom as those gathered feared the worst—that the jury would have to be discharged and the trial delayed while a new jury was found and sworn in.

The judge decided against taking this course of action and dismissed the juror.

'Justice must not only be done but it must be seen to be done,' he said by way of explanation.

'The presumption of innocence is a fundamental element of our system of justice.'

He also acknowledged the presence of journalists at the trial, at least two dozen, and he advised the jury members not to read any newspaper reports or listen to any news bulletins about the case.

'Somebody might get a distorted view of the emphasis of the case,' he explained before adding that his advice was for the 'purpose of keeping a clear and balanced mind'.

The first witness to be called to the stand was the topographer who painstakingly went through the various maps she had prepared of the areas concerned in the case. She was followed by a garda photographer from the Garda Technical Bureau who had taken shots of every angle of the murder scene and the couple's home in Naul.

As the jury members flicked through his books of photographs, the prosecution asked the photographer if he had taken shots at any other time connected with the case.

There was utter silence in the courtroom as he told how he had photographed a letter Joe had written to Rachel after her death and placed it in her coffin. The letter had been exhumed with Rachel's body.

Dominic McGinn, another barrister for the prosecution, read it out to the court.

Dated 8 October 2004, it read:

> Rachel, I love you so very, very much. I cannot think what I will ever do without you and I don't want to think. You are the best thing that ever happened to me and you will never be replaced.
>
> This is the hardest letter I've ever had to write for reasons only we know. Rachel, forgive me. Two words, one sentence. But I will say them forever.
>
> I look at Luke and I see you and hear you and smell you. I remember you. You have touched the lives of so many and made us better people. You made me laugh, you always did. Everyone loves you now and they always will.
>
> You were a smoker. You kept that quiet fair play to you. I am sorry about your mum finding out about Theresa, Thomas and co. But please don't blame me, it wasn't my fault.
>
> I miss you so much Rachie. Please, please remember that. You went away from this world so very young.

The world will remember how beautiful you were. Like Peter Pan you will never grow old.

Softball misses you, hockey is after naming a trophy after you. Everyone misses your mad personality and can do attitude.

Liam is heartbroken, your family, my family, everybody. Please look out for Jackie, your family and our boys. I need you as well.

Happy 31st birthday. You're no doubt having the best wine, the best coffee and the best ciggies.

Rachel I love you and miss you and I will mourn you forever.

XXX

Your hubby wubby Jofes.

Love you mammy, Luke XXX

Love you mammy, Adam XXX

As the letter from a man written to his murdered wife was read out, it was to be the first and only time during the entire trial that Joe showed even the slightest hint of emotion.

The captivated courtroom stared at him as they listened to the words he had written to Rachel. And under the gaze of the one hundred or so people gathered, Joe's face visibly reddened, he shifted uncomfortably in his seat and rubbed at his eyes, wiping away a tear or two.

It took several minutes for Joe to compose himself, while the rest of the courtroom, most of whom were hearing the contents of the infamous letter for the first time, digested the words.

The prosecution team then began calling ancillary witnesses.

John Doyle, a consultant meteorologist, was called on to give evidence that 4 October 2004 had been a mostly sunny day with a few scattered showers, a fact that was to prove vital towards the end of the trial.

A teacher and headmaster of Hedgestown primary school where Rachel and Joe's son Luke attended were the final witnesses of the day.

The following day Rose was called to the witness stand. It was an immensely measured and dignified appearance. She explained in a steady voice how as soon as she heard Rachel had not collected her son Adam from the crèche she had sensed something was wrong and insisted on calling out to her daughter's home.

She described arriving at the house, walking through the rooms calling her daughter's name and she told in chilling detail how she found Rachel's lifeless body in her bedroom and how she knew straight away she was dead.

It was a powerful testimony, all the more effective because of Rose's composure, the only time she even threatened to break down was when she described what Rachel was wearing, grey leggings and a grey t-shirt, her feet were bare.

Other witnesses called that day included Fr Stephen Redmond who gave absolution to Rachel after spotting the ambulance on the road. There were also several mothers who had children at the Tots United Montessori school and who saw Rachel that morning as she dropped Adam off.

The local milkman was next. He told how he had delivered milk at around 10am that day and had seen

Rachel's car parked in the driveway. He also noticed the curtains were pulled, which he said 'was not normal'.

Rachel's brother then took to the stand and explained how he was the first of the Callaly family that Joe contacted that day to tell them Rachel had not collected Adam from the crèche.

'I was extremely close to Rachel and Joe and the two kids,' he told the jury.

'I used to go out and spend long weekends. I spent a lot of time out there. And I had a good relationship with Joe, we both love cinema and going to the pictures. I have a lot of good memories from out there.'

Rachel's best friend Jackie Connor also made an impressively composed witness as she told the court of her close and lengthy relationship with the victim. She had last seen Rachel alive the Friday before on 1 October.

'I called in on my way home after a nightshift, that morning,' Jackie said.

'She was getting the boys ready for school and getting their breakfast. I was giving her money for Avon and Tupperware products as well. She was an agent for both. Joe wasn't there, he was in work. She was in fairly good spirits though a bit tired as she'd stayed up watching telly the night before.'

She then went through the day of the murder, which also happened to be her birthday. How Joe had rung her to ask her if Rachel was at her house and how she had headed out to the house in Naul, worried about her friend.

She described going down to her friend's bedroom, and how she checked for any signs of life but could find none. Jackie also noticed a cardboard box in Luke and Adam's room.

'There was a box in the boys' room,' she said. 'The bottom of it was covered in blood. Joe told me he had moved it to get closer to Rachel.'

She also gave the court the first glimpse into the true state of the couple's marriage.

'Rachel said she was not happy,' Jackie explained. 'She told me their family life was suffering because Joe was working a lot and she felt on her own.'

As well as the day of the murder, the witnesses also gave testimony about the days and weeks following Rachel's death. It became clear that the prosecution was building up a profile of Joe that showed his behaviour was not what you would expect from a normal grieving widower.

Jackie told how she went to a birthday party for Adam on 24 October 2004 and that Joe had asked her to go back to his mother's house in Dunleer for a chat.

'He said he was afraid he was going to be framed for murder,' Jackie told the hushed courtroom.

'You are going to have to help me prove my innocence.'

She said she was shocked and had asked him how he could be framed if he had an alibi. He replied: 'There are a few hours that are not accounted for where Rachel was.'

Another witness was Michelle Mulligan. She had been a good friend of Rachel's and her children went to the same school as Luke. She was at the Callaly's house the night people were writing notes to Rachel to place in her coffin and had a conversation with Joe about what more could be done to catch her killer.

'Joe said he'd suggested a number of things to the guards like going to the media and telling his story for as long as it was needed—until a person was caught. I said to him that it might not be such a good idea for you because you're such a big guy they might point the finger at you.

'Joe also said that whoever had done it would have scratches on him, Rachel was such a big strong girl, she'd put up a fight. Joe said he'd been checked for scratches.'

But perhaps some of the strangest conversations he had in the weeks after the murder were with Naomi Gargan, whose children went to school with the boys. She told how she met Joe at the crèche while he was dropping Adam off. After sympathising with him on his loss, she offered to help with the boys if he was ever stuck.

A little while later, Joe invited Naomi's daughter to the birthday party he had for his son Adam at the Leisureplex in Coolock. Naomi noticed that no member of Rachel's family was at the party but she was introduced to a woman called Nikki.

A week later, Naomi invited the O'Reilly boys to her son's birthday party at her house.

'Joe came to collect them. I was complaining about pains in my arms, he said "I have some dumb-bells you could use,"' she explained.

'To be honest I was kind of taken aback because there was speculation in the newspapers that it [the murder weapon] was a dumb-bell. It was a bit of a shock.'

At a later date Joe asked Naomi if she could collect his children from school as he had a meeting with his solicitor. As she passed the boys over to Joe he told her that he was going to be arrested.

'And he said: "I'm going to be held for 12 hours, just in case you think you've had a murderer in your house,"' Naomi told the courtroom.

'And he then told me: "They are following me, they are reading my text messages. Seemingly I am having an affair and you could be the one I'm having the affair with, don't be surprised if you're brought in for questioning."'

Naomi explained how she panicked after this last meeting with Joe and went home 'very upset' to her husband.

'I didn't want to get involved. I thought I was doing a good thing,' she said.

'I then heard on the news that a man had been arrested and I texted Joe to say that was great news.'

She said that Joe texted her later to say that his friends Derek and Nikki had been arrested: 'Derek was his alibi and Nikki was the woman I met at the party,' she explained.

Over the next couple of days, others told of their experiences with Joe in the weeks after Rachel's murder.

Rachel's brother Paul had called out to the O'Reilly home mid-November.

'I brought Anthony [his brother] out to Beldarragh to do a bit of painting,' he explained.

'Joe's sister, her boyfriend Dan, Joe and a friend of Joe's were also there. We didn't do any painting, after about an hour we sat down and watched TV, Manchester United were playing Arsenal.'

He went on to recount a conversation he had with Joe about a CCTV camera at Murphy's Quarry, which was less than half a mile away from the house.

'He asked me had I heard anything about how the investigation was going,' Paul explained.

'He was sitting opposite the window that looks out on Murphy's Quarry.

I said I hadn't really heard anything except that there was a camera and I asked Joe where it was in the Quarry.

'He said he didn't know about it, that he used to bring the kids up there and said if he had known about it he would have objected. I thought that was strange because if I had known about the camera I would have been happy.'

Rachel's friend, Fiona Slevin, had attended the funeral on 11 October and had gone to the reception afterwards at The Regency Hotel.

'I went to leave with friends and on the way out I saw Joe O'Reilly sitting with his mother, his sister and her boyfriend,' she told the court.

'He asked me to stay, that he hadn't spoken to me yet, so I stayed till 6pm.

'There was a discussion about the murder weapon. He [Joe] said: "I don't know why they're searching in the fields, it's in the water."

'I was shocked and his reaction then was like he'd said something wrong. And he said: "If I'd done it that's where it would be, because there's water all around and it would get rid of DNA and all that sort of stuff."

Another friend of Rachel's, Helen Reddy, then took the stand and explained how she had talked to Joe on the night of the murder. 'He had called me earlier to tell me Rachel was dead,' she said. 'We had a conversation about whether she had been sexually assaulted. I asked him if she had been and he said absolutely no way.'

Joe's colleague at Viacom, Michelle Slattery, told how Joe had arrived into the office on the day of the murder at around noon and made a cup of coffee.

She said his face was puffy and bloated and red and his eyes were the same.

'He looked like he had been crying,' she said. 'I hadn't seen him like that before so I presumed he had been crying. I said to him: "Jesus you look like shit." He shrugged his shoulders and went "Oh Jesus."'

The court also began to hear from a selection of garda officers who had worked on the murder case.

Detective Jeanette O'Neill told how the team entered the murder scene together at around 6.20pm after the photographer had finished his work.

'The kitchen was in a dishevelled state,' she explained.

'There was a lack of daylight so it was decided to keep the body where it was until the following morning. We didn't want to miss any evidence.

'Through my observations, the victim had sustained a violent assault while at the house in Beldarragh, primarily in the main bedroom of the property.'

The detective also examined Rachel's car. 'There were two baby seats in the back and we found Rachel's rucksack and a diary. It was very messy, strewn with rubbish and clothes.'

Detective Shane Henry said they found thirty different areas of blood splatters at the scene, which included one on the ceiling between the main bedroom and the children's bedroom, and one on the ceiling directly over the body.

He also observed that the washing machine was set at a 40 degree wash cycle and the clothes inside were clean and slightly damp.

Garda Rory Keating told how he had examined the kitchen area and had found €860 untouched in a plastic container on a ledge in the utility room. A handbag which contained €450 was also found in the house that was presumed to have been targeted by burglars.

Another officer, Garda Thomas Cleary, was tasked with keeping unauthorised people out of the crime scene while it was being examined. He testified that Joe had told him he had moved a box out of the way to get nearer Rachel's body. 'He said he'd come into contact with her body,' explained the officer. 'And he said: "I'm really sorry, I'm probably after ruining it [the murder scene] on you.'

Garda Damien O'Connell was one of the first officers on the scene the day of the murder when he observed, 'Presses at the house were pulled open and contents were strewn about, the kitchen table was at an angle.

'I noticed blood on the walls of the hall and on the floor,' he added.

'I saw a female lying on the ground, she appeared to be lifeless. There was a pool of blood directly under her head on the carpet.'

He told how he returned to the house five days later, on 9 October when a garda team was sent to carry out a detailed search of the house for more evidence.

'Mr O'Reilly asked me who they were,' the officer told the court. 'He told me to get them to check the room . . . beside where Rachel was found, that he had weights in that room and one of them could have been the murder weapon.'

The gardaí also carried out a search of the area surrounding the house in which they found two bags, a leather satchel with a flight tag attached with the name O'Reilly on it and a camera bag in a nearby ditch.

'It was about .4 of a mile from the house on the left-hand side of the road,' explained Garda Nicola Sheeran.

'They [the bags] were sitting on top of the water, just sitting there, placed there. They were clearly visible from the road.'

And she said that as her colleague, Inspector Oliver Keegan, picked the bags out of the water a white jewellery box fell out.

Garda Edmund Sheridan was part of the team who searched the O'Reilly house.

'We found a mobile telephone in the pocket of a red jacket,' he said.

'There was also a petrol blue jacket and a hand towel in the bathroom that was wet. There was clothing in the washing machine, both kids and adults—a man's pink shirt, a purple shirt, grey trousers and navy trousers.'

Dr Diane Daly, the forensic scientist, was able to determine from studying the blood splatter at the murder scene that Rachel had been beaten repeatedly. She said it was likely the killer had been crouched or kneeling during the attack and that her head had been moved afterwards.

'Her head and hair were heavily bloodstained; there was a heavy pooling of blood in one area,' she explained.

'There was a lot of low level blood splatter. In my opinion she was violently beaten for a sustained length of time while lying on the floor.'

She also said that part of the floor near the body did not have any blood on it.

'The void in the blood stain—a possible explanation is that the assailant was crouching or kneeling in the area.'

For members of the Callaly family the technical description of how Rachel was beaten to death was too gruesome to bear and stifled sobs could be heard coming from their bench.

Dr Daly went on to detail how blood was found on the front door of the washing machine, but it was not Joe's. She added that no blood was found on the clothes from the washing machine that she was given to examine.

'That may not be significant if the clothes were washed,' she said.

The forensic scientist told how she was given over 100 items from the scene to examine, including the clothes Rachel was wearing that day, samples from her body including hair, nail cuttings, swabs from her hands and feet and a set of keys that had been found under her body.

Dr Daly said there were no traces of semen found anywhere. She did, however, find three tiny blood stains on Joe's right boot but there was no other blood found on the rest of his clothes or in his car.

There was also blood found on Rose Callaly's runner.

James McNally is a dairy farmer with land directly opposite the O'Reilly's home. Unable to make Rachel's funeral, he met Joe on 15 October and offered his condolences.

He too gave evidence.

'I told him I was very sorry I didn't go to the funeral and I sympathised with him on his loss,' McNally told the court.

'He asked me if I had seen anything that morning. I said that I had actually; my son and I met a red car. He said, "Oh yes, that was a red Mercedes, the guards traced that car."

'It was definitely not a Mercedes,' McNally said firmly.

'In my opinion it was a red Ford Escort. A week or two after the 15th I was having a general conversation with Joe. During the course of the conversation I asked him, "Who do you think did it?" He answered: "We're all suspects, you're a suspect, I'm a suspect."

'I smiled and said, "I know where I was."'

Tara Kennedy, an army sergeant, grew up with Rachel and had gone to the same school but explained she had not been that close to her at the time of her death.

'We had a lot of contact before she was married, I was at the wedding but we lost contact after she was married.'

Tara went to Rachel's funeral where she was involved in a conversation with Joe that left her feeling distinctly uncomfortable.

'We had various conversations but something stuck in my mind,' she explained. 'He said: "It's ironic, here we were at the church at 10am and she had been killed at 10.05am and here we are at 2pm [at the reception] when the body was found at 2.10pm.

'I felt shocked at these words, I just remember looking at my feet. I just lifted my head and went on to change the subject to Star Wars. I knew that Star Wars was a big hobby of his, I knew he had a room dedicated to Star Wars in the house. I just wanted to change the subject.'

Another childhood friend of Rachel's, Sarah Kiernan, also remembered the same conversation and told how she had felt 'uneasiness' and that it was 'inappropriate'.

The prosecution then began to call witnesses who had seen Joe on the morning of the murder. From the receptionist who worked at the gym where Joe and his work colleague Quearney went at 6.40am, to a long list of Viacom employees who spotted the pair in the office at various stages throughout the day.

Tracy O'Neill was an operations assistant who worked for Joe and Quearney and was able to tell the court that they both carried out inspections to make sure advertisements were being placed by the bill posters.

'The southside usually by Derek and the north-side usually by Joe,' she explained. 'Sometimes they did them together, they sometimes travelled together, sometimes separately; it depended on the day.'

Damian Tully was employed to paste posters on buses by Viacom. He explained that on 4 October he was told he was covering for a colleague who was on holidays and so instead of Broadstone bus depot he was sent to a dart station in the city centre where his company van was clamped.

Noel Paget was instead sent to Broadstone by Quearney and he arrived there at 10.15am, but because the buses he needed to work on were elsewhere, he went into the canteen for some much-needed breakfast to settle his 'slight hangover'.

He got a phone call at around mid-day and was told to go elsewhere. He was positive that he didn't see Joe or Quearney that morning at Broadstone.

Other staff from Viacom were called to give evidence. The company's managing director Phillip Brown told of a conversation he had with Joe over lunch at the Shelbourne Hotel on 26 October. Brown insisted his chat about Rachel's murder with Joe, who had started working for Viacom in 2002, was still 'fairly clear' in his mind.

'He had one or two suspicions,' Browne explained. 'He suspected it may have been a man from NLT, who he had asked to install an alarm, and he was querying why the police were not questioning him. He was convinced the killer knew Rachel.

'He said it [the crime scene] was very, very messy, that there was a lot of blood and that he had embraced

Joe O'Reilly met Rachel Callaly when she was just 17-years-old. The two complimented each other physically as both were unusually tall—Joe stood 6ft 5in tall while Rachel was 5ft 11in.

Joe and Rachel's wedding photos show a young and attractive couple, who appeared to be deeply in love and excited at the idea of spending the rest of their lives together.

They both played softball, and participated in the longest continuous game of softball in the world, which got them into the Guinness Book of World Records.

Above: Joe and Rachel in happier times.

Right: Rachel's mother and sister, Rose and Anne Callaly, outside Rachel's home near Naul during a memorial service two years after her death.

Below: Lambay View, the day after Rachel's murder. It had been her dream home with a massive garden and distant sea views.

© Colin Keegan/ Collins Agency

© Colin Keegan/ Collins Agency

© Image courtesy of RTE

Above: The public first became aware of bad feeling between Joe and Rachel's family, the Callalys, during an appearance on *The Late Late Show* three weeks after Rachel's death when it was claimed that Rose was openly cold towards her son-in-law.

Below: Joe pictured kneeling in a Garda van at the Court House in Swords after being charged with Rachel's murder.

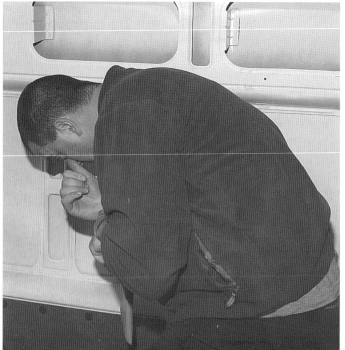

© Tom Honan

© Tom Honan

© Joe Dunne

Above and previous page: Joe outside Swords court house having been charged with Rachel's murder. There was unprecedented media coverage of his trial.

Left: Joe with his mother, Ann, who attended the Central Criminal Court each day of his trial.

Below: Joe in an unmarked Garda car, after being arrested at his home in Naul.

© Lindsay Campbell   © Seán Dwyer

Above: Derek Quearney, who worked with Joe at Viacom, gave evidence in the trial.

Rachel's biological mother, Theresa Lowe (above left) attended the trial, anxious to see justice done for her first born child. Her half-brother, Thomas Lowe (centre), gave evidence at the trial, as did Joe's mistress, Nikki Pelley (right).

© Michael Chester

Tears of joy and sorrow as the Callaly family celebrate Joe O'Reilly's conviction.

© Michael Chester

Joe being taken to prison to begin his life sentence on 21 July 2007, the day he was found guilty of his wife's murder.

his wife. He was conscious he may have contaminated the evidence.'

Neighbours of the O'Reillys, Kevin and Maura Moore, had been named by Joe as people who might have had a grudge against Rachel.

They both admitted that Rachel had raised an issue with them over the boundary of their properties but said there had been no conflict between them. In fact, according to Maura Moore, she got on very well with Rachel. 'She was a lady, she was very nice,' said Moore before explaining that Rachel came to see her about maps she had drawn up of her property.

'She just called out. It was a summer's afternoon and she came into the kitchen. She said she had a problem. She was very embarrassed.'

Rachel told Moore that her solicitor said their title maps showed their lands went further on paper than the section that had been fenced off. Moore said that she had worked in a solicitor's office for 25 years and told Rachel she did not think there was a problem.

'I said to her the house had changed hands since I had lived there. If there had been a problem it would have arisen before that. She apologised twice. I said to her to get the maps. Kevin was reared in the area and he was very familiar with it. We left on good terms. She apologised and said she was embarrassed. She said Joe just asked her to come and get it cleared up.'

For the first time a friend of Joe's was called to the stand and it was made very clear that Joe and Rachel's marriage had been far from happy. In fact Joe had been planning on leaving his wife, according to his close friend John Austin.

He told the court that he had met Joe playing soft-ball and had struck up a 'close relationship' with him. He had also 'got to know Rachel reasonably well.'

He went on to explain that his own marriage had broken down in 2004 and he had separated from his wife. It was perhaps only natural that Joe had opened his heart to Austin about his own domestic issues.

'He told me they were having marital difficulties,' said Austin, who runs his own electronic branding company. 'And that they were sleeping in separate bedrooms.'

He said Joe had also discussed the possibility of moving out of the family home in Beldarragh and into his own apartment. 'From my recollection he wanted to get one in Balbriggan so he could be close to the kids,' said an obviously uncomfortable Austin. 'I would categorise him as a very caring father, yes.'

As the questioning continued, the name Nikki Pelley was mentioned again.

Austin revealed how on the 8 September 2004 he had held a dinner party at his partner's home in Dublin.

'There was myself and my partner, Joe and Nikki Pelley,' he said.

For several minutes the prosecution quizzed Austin about Pelley's connection to the accused.

'I would categorise her as a close friend of Joe's,' said Austin.

'How close?' asked the prosecution.

'In fairness it's difficult to say,' was the reply.

'There was little conversation in terms of how close they were. But if you're asking me did I ever see any intimacy between them, then no.'

The prosecution tried another tack.

'Did you think they were only platonic friends?'

'No,' was the short and final reply.

❖ ❖ ❖ ❖ ❖

Just one of the unpleasant twists of the case included Rachel's birth brother Thomas Lowe being questioned closely by the defence about his movements on the day of the murder. A trace of his blood had been found on the washing machine in the O'Reilly home but he had been ruled out as a suspect.

The carpenter told the court he had cut his hand with a saw while he was helping to build decking in Rachel's back garden in August 2004.

'I went into the house to wash my hand and went into the utility room to get a dressing,' he said.

'I put the dressing on myself and some of the blood went on to the washing machine. I told Rachel but she said not to worry that she'd clean it up so I went back to work.'

The defence then pointed out that Lowe had not mentioned the incident to the gardaí until five months after the murder.

'I wouldn't have thought it was important at the time, to tell you the truth,' he replied.

He also explained how Rachel used to keep a key outside the back patio door and that he had brought it up a number of times with her because he didn't think it was a good idea. But he said Rachel had always assured him that it was 'completely safe'.

Lowe was again quizzed about whether or not he was anywhere near the O'Reilly home on the day of the murder. He said he woke up that morning when his brother Patrick rang him to say he couldn't make it to work. Lowe explained that two people were needed for the job, so he went back to bed until 12.30pm.

He said the first person who saw him that day was a woman who was doing a church collection.

The prosecution then asked him if he had gone out to the O'Reilly home on the morning of 4 October 2004.

'No I didn't,' he replied.

'Did you see Rachel O'Reilly that day?'

Again Lowe answered firmly: 'No I didn't.'

Finished giving his testimony and clearly distressed, Lowe quickly made his way out of Court 2.

It marked the end of the first week of Joe's murder trial.

CHAPTER 7

Dramas, Dreams and Mobile Phones

BY 2 JULY 2007, six days into the trial, more than 80 witnesses had been called, but the prosecution's case was far from complete. The prosecution had yet to establish a motive.

Those attending the courtroom every day wondered if the initial estimation of a six-week trial was possibly a little optimistic. And despite its being the second week of evidence, there was no sign of interest in the trial waning. If anything it was attracting more attention with each passing day.

The trial was threatened with collapse for a second time when it emerged that a Book of Evidence had found its way into the jury room.

The trial judge, however, decided the case should continue.

The Book of Evidence contained all witness statements taken by the investigation team, some of which would never be heard by the jury.

How the documents ended up in the jury room was never explained. Before deciding to continue with the trial, Justice White asked the jury: 'Did any one of you read anything in that Book of Evidence, any portion or any statement?'

The tension in the courtroom was palpable. Dismissing the jury and starting again would have meant the entire trial would be rescheduled and proceed the following year.

The idea that the devastated Callalys would have to wait yet again for the suspect of Rachel's murder to be tried was torturous. Already they looked drained and exhausted.

Each jury member shook their head and replied no.

'I'm obliged to make this inquiry,' said Justice White. 'I am not casting any dispersions.'

He ruled, however, that the trial should continue, but not before asking both the prosecution and defence if there were any objections.

They both said no.

The trial continued and several of Joe's colleagues from Viacom were called.

The suspect's friend, Kieran Gallagher, a bank official with AIB, provided a more personal insight into the lives of the O'Reillys. He explained how he met the couple playing softball and became friendly with Joe. He told how Joe had confided in him a couple of months before the murder that he and Rachel were having marital difficulties.

'We were having lunch and Joe discussed that they were having marital problems but that they were seeing a counsellor,' he said. 'There was something to do with Rachel being snappy with the children.'

The witness went on to reveal that Joe had told him someone had reported Rachel to the social services. The bank worker was asked if he knew who had reported her but he said he didn't.

Before he stepped down he explained how he was supposed to meet Joe for lunch on the afternoon of the murder but had to cancel as his daughter was ill.

Next it was the turn of the State Pathologist to take the stand. It made for a grim couple of hours as Dr Marie Cassidy told the court that from her examination of Rachel's body, it appeared that the mother-of-two had tried to defend herself from her attacker and may have clung on to life for hours after she was savagely beaten.

In her soft Scottish accent, the pathologist detailed how Rachel was struck 'several times' on the head, fracturing her skull. But these injuries, inflicted by a blunt object, did not kill her instantly.

'She could have lain unconscious for some few hours prior to her dying,' Dr Cassidy explained.

And she told how the beating sustained by Rachel was so savage that she was unable to tell precisely how many blows had been inflicted.

There were eight lacerations to the head and 'depending on the weapon used, these could have been caused by a minimum of four separate blows, but could also have been caused by up to nine separate blows.'

The first blow, to the top of Rachel's head, was not fatal but could have given her a concussion, and the injuries to the forehead indicated that she could have been standing upright when the first blow was struck.

The pathologist found several bruises on Rachel's arms. 'She [Rachel] appeared to make some attempt to defend herself as the injuries to her arms were defensive,' Dr Cassidy said.

Marks to her neck indicated Rachel might have been gripped in an arm lock, and a bruise on her wrist suggested it might have been gripped tightly.

Also an injury to Rachel's mouth indicated she might have received a blow to the face.

And like Dr Daly before her, Dr Cassidy told how the attacker repeatedly hit Rachel over the head as she lay on the floor.

'These were forceful and heavy blows from a weapon, most likely inflicted as she was lying on the ground,' she said.

Listening intently to the horrific details of their sister's death, Anne, Declan and Anthony Callaly were deeply affected by what they heard. As Declan sat with his head bowed, Anne was comforted by an aunt. Anthony covered his face with his hand and his girlfriend put her arm around him in an effort to soothe his pain. Eventually it all became too much and the couple quietly left the courtroom before the pathologist stepped down.

In the meantime, this vivid evidence prompted another rare flash of emotion from the accused.

Leaning forward with his face resting on his hand, Joe stared straight ahead. Several times he swallowed hard as he listened to the injuries that had been inflicted on his wife of 12 years. Those sitting close to him were certain his eyes welled up, and there was a point where it looked as though he was wiping away a tear.

But it was not over yet.

'While unconscious she would have inhaled blood,' Dr Cassidy continued and added that there was a fracture to the right side and back of the skull consistent with bleeding and damage to the brain, and there was extensive bruising to the right side of the face.

'In my opinion,' the pathologist added, 'the eventual cause of death was blunt force trauma to her head, inhalation of blood, scalp lacerations, skull fractures and brain contusion.'

She also said her temperature test gave a loose suggestion of the time of death and Rachel could have died anytime between 9am and 3pm.

'It just gives a rough indication of when death occurred,' she explained. 'In some cases it can be useless. In this case it gave a very wide margin.'

Another result from Dr Cassidy's post mortem was that there was no evidence of sexual assault, just as Joe had told Rachel's friend, Helen Reddy, on the day of the murder.

It emerged that reporters were not the only people Joe brought on what one newspaper dubbed 'gruesome murder tours' of his house. Over the next couple of days, friends and relatives testified that he had insisted on taking them to the bedroom where he demonstrated how he believed Rachel had been killed.

The jury was sent out while the legal teams debated whether or not this evidence should be admitted. The judge agreed to listen to the testimonies of those involved before making his decision.

Rachel's mother Rose was the first who told how Joe called out to her home on 13 October 2004 to tell them he had got the keys back from the gardaí for the house in Naul. He wondered if Rose and Jimmy would like to come up for a look.

Rose said she felt uneasy but agreed to go up with Jimmy, their son, Paul, and his wife Denise to collect some of Rachel's belongings.

Walking into the house, Joe asked the four Callalys if they would like to hear the messages that had been left on the landline's answering service on the day Rachel was murdered.

Rose said that nobody answered him, but Joe kept insisting they listen to the messages.

'I remember there were a good few calls on it. While we were listening to the calls I was asking myself why he was doing it?' Rose told the court.

But Joe's odd behaviour did not end there. He then insisted on bringing the small group down to the bedroom where Rachel had been killed.

'The room was still in the same state it was when the body was taken away,' Rose said.

'There was blood everywhere. Joe was looking at the blood spatter and making remarks.

'Joe raised his right arm and said she must have got a blow and fallen. He actually got down on his hunkers and repeatedly made a striking action where her head had been. He said that when he [the killer] got her down he made sure she didn't get up again.'

Rose then demonstrated to the court how Joe had made the striking motion. 'He kept making these movements,' she said.

'He kept saying he [the killer] must have done this and must have done that. He was seemingly going through how she was murdered.'

Her husband Jimmy was also unhappy about going to the house that day.

'He [Joe] rang and asked did we want to go down to Rachel's house to see it. I was shocked. I didn't want to go,' Jimmy explained.

'He said when he went into the house he felt an inner peace and he felt Rachel was there.'

Again Jimmy said he was shocked when Joe asked them if they wanted to listen to the phone recordings.

'He more or less insisted on playing it,' he said. 'As he was playing it he looked at our faces to see our reactions. It was very odd.'

Clearly distressed at the memory, Jimmy then told how Joe had insisted on acting out how he thought Rachel had been attacked.

'He got down on his hunkers and he kept hitting her and saying look at the blood here and here,' said Jimmy.

'I nearly got sick. I just felt I was going to pass out. I think I moved away up the hall.'

Rachel's brother Paul recounted how Joe seemed to have 'a thing' about listening to the phone messages. 'None of us were interested,' Paul said. 'We were all looking for Rachel's clothes to take them away and wash them.' And he said he remembered Joe asking them: 'Are yis ready for this?'

'He pretty much stuck it on without any of us answering.'

Paul also gave a detailed account of Joe's peculiar re-enactment of Rachel's death.

'He started pointing at blood splatters on the wall,' Paul explained.

'He was indicating someone must have hit Rachel like that [as he made a striking motion] and that was how the blood got there.'

Joe then got down on one knee and made another striking motion before walking to the bathroom to where he pointed out a drop of blood that was still on the floor.

'He said: "They [the killer] must have stopped here and the blood would have dripped off the weapon. They must have heard her make noise, a groan or whatever,"' said Paul.

For Paul's wife Denise, the memory of that day was almost too distressing to recount.

'Joe was standing in Rachel's bedroom. He went down on one knee and had his fist clenched tightly,' she said before bursting into tears.

'He made a striking action, like he was hitting Rachel on the ground,' she finally continued.

'He was commenting on the low splatter of blood on the wall.'

According to Denise, Joe then crossed over into the bathroom with his fist still clenched.

'He said they [the killer] would have heard her moaning. He left the bathroom and came back towards the bedroom,' Denise tearfully explained. 'Just outside the bedroom at the saddle of the door he got down on one knee again and hit his fist off the ground. He said they came back to finish her off.'

Joe also re-enacted the murder for his long-term friend Alan Boyle.

In his statement to the gardaí, Boyle told how Joe pointed out spatters of blood on the walls and offered to show him how he thought she was killed. Joe told his friend that he believed the killer had waited in the bedroom for Rachel. And he showed Boyle the position Rachel's body was found in on the ground and knelt down and did a striking motion.

'He was very calm about it all, very matter of fact, which I found unusual,' Boyle admitted.

'But then I don't know what way people in grief react.'

He said they then went back to the kitchen to have a cup of tea and began to go through the possibilities of who could have done it. Boyle told how he had suggested to Joe that Rachel might have been having an affair and the killer could have been a jealous boyfriend.

Boyle, who had known the couple as long as they had known each other, said he was totally shocked by the reaction to his question.

'Joe said that he couldn't give a fuck what Rachel had got up to,' Boyle said. 'Later on I found out indirectly from his mother that he had a fling, but it was only once.

'I said to Joe that all the gardaí had was circumstantial, but that if they got something else I would have difficulty believing you.'

According to Boyle, his friend replied: 'When you stop believing me, let me know.'

Rachel's best friend, Jackie Connor, was also called back to the stand while the jury was out to give evidence about a dream Joe told her he had. She had been visiting him at his mother's house when he recounted yet another story.

'He said he had laid down in the spot where Rachel had died and she had come to him in a dream,' Jackie explained. But the conversation stopped when Joe's sister, Ann, came into the room.

Jackie resumed her conversation with Joe two days later at the O'Reilly's home in Naul.

'I was standing in the bedroom and Joe O'Reilly was standing in the hall close to me,' she said.

Joe told her that in the dream Rachel got two blows to the head and then the killer heard her gurgling or choking on her blood. The killer then went back and 'whacked her head'.

Joe then said to her that the dream was Rachel's way of showing him what happened from beyond the grave.

'He said they held her down, that's why blood splashed all around,' Jackie continued.

'He told me that he had told the gardaí there were two towels missing from the bathroom, one brown and one white. He said a weight, a bell bar, which was Joe's, was missing from the spare bedroom, where Joe slept.

'And he said he believed it was somebody Rachel trusted.'

He also told Jackie that whoever killed Rachel knew exactly what they were doing.

'He said the area behind the ear was the correct place to hit someone if you want to kill them,' Jackie told the court. 'He said someone with military training would know this.'

Joe also told Celine Keogh about Rachel appearing to him in a dream.

'[In the dream] he said he was drawn toward the window of the spare room and that Rachel was saying, "Think, Joe." This was the room where he kept his weights. He said it came to him that it was a weight that was the murder weapon,' Keogh recounted.

Neighbour and friend Fidelma Geraghty had last seen Rachel a week or so before her death when they shared a pizza and some wine at the O'Reilly's home. That night Rachel had given Geraghty a present of an incense set and a plant, but she had forgotten to take them with her.

Geraghty told the court that she wanted something to remember Rachel by, so on 2 November, she called back to the house to collect the presents.

'Joe was there and there was another guy with him, Ciaran and his wife Jennifer,' she told the court.

'Joe answered the door to me and invited me in. I didn't want to come in because of what happened, but Joe insisted. Joe said people felt at peace when they came in.'

Geraghty said she chatted to Jennifer for a while but then, 'Joe said he would give me the tour.'

'I said, "No," that I didn't want to. He responded that a lot of people found it peaceful.'

She told how Joe had brought her down to the bedroom and was talking 'about the forensics and what he had to do for the guards'.

She said Joe began to point at the blood stains on the walls and showed her where a large section of carpet had been cut out because it was saturated with blood. He then re-enacted the murder for her.

'He went to the bedroom,' explained Geraghty.

'I was standing at the door. He said Rachel was possibly bending down to get something from the table in the bedroom. [He said] that she was hit from the back and to the side.'

Joe then 'got down on the floor' to show how the killer repeatedly hit Rachel as she lay on the ground.

'[He said] they went into the bathroom to take a shower and they heard her moan and they went back to finish her off,' Geraghty said.

'I was flabbergasted. I could not understand how he was talking about that.'

Joe also quizzed her about the CCTV cameras at Murphy's Quarry near his house. He told her that newspapers had reported the gardaí had obtained footage from it.

'He asked me if I knew what type of CCTV cameras they were,' she said. 'Why they were pointing down at the house and could you get a reg plate of a car from them.

'I said I didn't know for certain how good it was or it wasn't.'

Another neighbour, Sarah Harmon, recounted her own strange encounter with Joe, which happened a week or so after he got the keys for his house back.

Sarah brought her three-and-a-half-year-old daughter Sophie with her as she visited Joe to see how he was bearing up.

Joe asked her if she wanted to go and see the bedroom where Rachel was murdered. She left Sophie in the kitchen with him as she went down to the room alone.

'I sat on the bed. I was quite upset,' she said. But then Joe appeared at the bedroom door.

'He got down on his knees in the bedroom where the underlining was cut from the carpet,' she said.

'Using his left hand he showed the blood spatter on the wall and said this must have been Rachel's blood and with his right hand he did the same and said this must be the killer's blood.

'He said they [the killer] must have been short and they must have beat her repeatedly. He moved his hand down from his head quite violently. I was shocked by the physicality of the situation. I found it quite hard to deal with.'

She told how her daughter Sophie then appeared at the door and she didn't want her to come into the room, so Joe picked the little girl up and put her into Luke and Adam's room across the hall.

Joe then began showing her blood spots on the wall that gardaí had ringed with biro.

'I switched off at that stage. I did not want to take anymore in,' Sarah told the court.

Several of Rachel's other friends were also treated to Joe's accounts of what might have happened to his wife.

Bríd Horan spoke to him two days after the murder at the Callalys' house. She was there with her sister Helen Reddy, her friend Celine Keogh and one or two other friends when someone brought up the injuries that had been inflicted on Rachel.

'He [Joe] raised his hand and pointed here, here and here [pointing at upper arms] and he also mentioned head injuries,' she said.

'I think he pointed to the right [of the back of the head]. He had mentioned that if you were going to kill someone that is where you would aim. He said not a lot of people would know that. A person would know that if they were in the army.'

Keogh recounted this particular conversation vividly.

'He said he had seen injuries to her head. He said Rachel would have got four or five blows to her head,' she said.

'He actually pointed with his hands to where they might be. He pointed to one behind the ears.

'He said that if he and another friend of ours, Pat Reddy, had wanted to kill someone, this is where they would have hit.'

Another one of the friends, Fiona Slevin, said Joe claimed the killer wanted the murder to look like a botched robbery.

'He told me there was blood all over the hall and the bedroom and that there were towels missing,' Fiona said.

'He felt it was staged. He felt the person who did it knew Rachel and that someone at the funeral was crying crocodile tears.'

It was bizarre behaviour by anyone's standards and the jury was sent out for four days while the defence and prosecution teams debated whether the re-enactments should be allowed into evidence.

Gageby fought hard to stop the re-enactments and other witness testimonies from being put before the jury.

'There was no particular secret knowledge required to make these particular statements,' he argued.

'Mr O'Reilly attended the scene and saw his wife's body and touched her.'

The barrister said that when the house was given back to Joe after gardaí were finished examining it, the bloodstains were still in the bedroom and hallway.

'How could anyone seeing the position of her body not conclude that she had suffered a terrible attack and that these injuries were inflicted where she lay?'

He also argued that many of the witnesses, 'especially the women,' the prosecution wanted to present to the jury showed 'visible emotion'.

And he accused the prosecution of trying to inject 'palpable emotion' into the trial.

Justice White agreed with the defence application and said he believed Joe would not have needed direct knowledge of the murder to carry out such re-enactments.

He ruled the evidence to be highly prejudicial. So the accounts of Joe's 'murder tours' were never presented to the jury. It was time to call the jury back.

✤ ✤ ✤ ✤ ✤

Detective Sergeant Patrick Marry, Detective Superintendent Michael Hoare and Sergeant Aaron

Gormley were the officers who called out to Joe's mother's house in Dunleer, where he was staying with his two sons on the night of the murder.

Only after being asked three times did Joe finally admit to having an affair with his work colleague, Nikki Pelley.

'He said the affair was over and he didn't want his family to know,' explained Marry.

Joe's first statement taken on 4 October 2004—in which he gave details of his affair—was read out to the court by Vaughan-Buckley.

'I would tell Rachel I would be sleeping in the office but I later began to stay at Nikki's on Tuesday. This later extended to Saturday evenings . . . Rachel knew nothing about Nikki except that I had a friend called Nikki.'

Joe explained that two or three weeks before the murder, he went to Nikki's house early in the morning instead of going to the gym. And that on the morning of Rachel's death, Nikki had phoned him but he decided not to call over to her.

She rang him again later and asked to meet him for lunch but he had already planned to meet Kieran Gallagher.

In the statement, he said the only person who knew about his relationship with Nikki was Quearney and that was because he had spotted them in a car together.

When asked that night if there was anyone he could think of who might hold a grudge against him or Rachel, Joe told the officers that there was a land dispute with neighbours. Though he also mentioned a Viacom employee he had recently sacked.

'He could have done it,' Joe told them.

His statement went on to detail how Rachel had been adopted by the Callalys but had made contact with her birth mother and brother, Theresa and Thomas Lowe, when she was 18. In recent times, however, 'Things were not too hot between them.'

The officers asked Joe about his own movements earlier that day and where he had been at the time of his wife's murder.

He told them he had been carrying out a bus inspection with his work colleague Quearney at the Broadstone depot in Phibsborough, just north of the city centre on the morning of the murder. He said they planned to check on the work of employee Damian Tully, whose job it was to put advertisements on the sides of buses.

Joe claimed they had left their office at Bluebell and travelled in separate cars because they could both claim mileage expense. He said he arrived at the depot at around 9am, but because there was no parking available inside, he left his car outside an apartment block across the road.

Joe said he couldn't find Tully so he went to another area in the depot and began inspecting some buses. The first and only contact he made with anyone at the garage that morning was around 9.30am when Quearney rang him to see where he was.

The two men, Joe claimed, then met up.

He said that he did not speak to the foreman of the depot at any stage but that Quearney did. In fact the only person Joe said he spoke to at Broadstone that morning was Quearney. And while they did come across Tully's van, he said there was no sign of the Viacom employee, and his mobile phone appeared to be in the van. Tully's absence was going to be discussed at a meeting later that day back in the office, Joe said.

At one stage, around 10am, he sent a text message to Rachel. 'It was just to see how she and the kids were,' he said before adding that it was about 11.30am by the time they had finished inspecting the buses.

He said they left Broadstone, again in their own cars, and arrived back in Viacom at about midday.

The prosecution now moved to dispel Joe's version of events by producing phone records for his mobile phone. These contradicted his account of his movements on the morning his wife was murdered.

It was to prove a fascinating lesson in the tracking capabilities of a mobile phone. Although such evidence had been used before in several other high-profile trials, it appeared Joe was unaware that any calls or texts to or from his phone would leave a trail.

In his detailed testimony, Oliver Farrell, an electronic engineer with Vilicom, an engineering consultant company, simplified the workings of the mobile phone network.

He explained how transmitters generate the signals needed to make a call from a mobile phone. These are positioned on telephone masts that are dotted around the country. Usually there are three to six transmitters on each of the masts, depending on the density of the population in the immediate area.

Each of the transmitters points in different direct-ions away from the mast in order to get full coverage. And when a person makes or receives a call or text on their mobile phone, he said it is routed through the mast that is providing the strongest signal, which is typically the one that is nearest.

This is how Farrell and his colleague Karim Benabdallah were both able to determine that Joe was not at the Broadstone depot at the time of Rachel's death, which is what he had claimed in his statement.

The court was brought through all the calls and texts made to and from Joe's mobile telephone on 4 October.

From the very first call he made that morning on his way to the gym at 5.25am to his message minder, routed through the Balheary base station in north Dublin, right through to a call he made to his sister Ann at 2.43pm, which was routed through the mast at Murphy's Quarry near his home and was just shortly after Rachel's body had been discovered.

But the two most important communications registered to his phone that day were at 9.25am and 9.52am, a period of time when Joe insisted he was at the Broadstone depot.

The prosecution outlined that he received a call from Quearney at 9.25am. However, this was routed through the Murphy's Quarry mast, which is just half a mile from the murder scene. The prosecution team also introduced evidence concerning a text he received 27 minutes later from Kieran Gallagher, which was to say he couldn't make lunch. This was also routed through the mast at Naul.

Benabdallah explained how he worked as a senior technical consultant with the mobile phone company O₂ Ireland. He said he had been requested to examine the coverage facilities of the base station at Murphy's Quarry.

When asked if it was possible that someone using a phone in the Broadstone depot would have their communication routed through the mast at Murphy's Quarry, he replied emphatically: 'It's impossible.'

Farrell was also requested to examine the calls made to and from Quearney's mobile phone that day to see if they corresponded with the movements he told gardaí he made. He was asked to see if Joe and Quearney's phones were in the same area at the times the accused said they were together.

His results revealed that the records of Quearney's mobile phone showed he was in the vicinity of Broadstone on the morning of the murder, which is what he told the gardaí.

But the first time activity on Joe's phone was routed through a mast near Broadstone was at 10:38am, an hour and 13 minutes after Quearney's phone was first used in the area.

Prior to this, Joe's phone had been used in a number of areas in north Dublin, which was contrary to what he had claimed in his statement.

A visual aid was provided to the court by Enda Furlong, a principal engineer with O₂ Ireland.

The movements of Joe and Quearney's phones that day were illustrated on a map of the greater Dublin area, shown on two large plasma screens on either side of the judge's bench.

As Joe's phone moved, coloured sections on the map lit up successively.

These showed the coverage area of the different mobile phone masts and you could clearly see how Joe's phone moved from an area served by the Killeen Road mast close to his office in the Bluebell Industrial Estate, right up to north Co Dublin.

And it crucially illustrated the two communications at 9.25am and 9.52am, which lit up the area covered by the Murphy's Quarry mast. A separate diagram showed how the station is located just 850 metres from the O'Reilly home.

A second presentation indicated the areas where Quearney's phone was used that morning and then compared them with the movements of Joe's phone between 7.30am and 12.01pm.

Using the colour blue for the areas where Joe's phone was used and red for Quearney's phone usage, it was clear that the two phones could not have been near each other for over an hour when Joe had claimed the two of them were together at Broadstone.

The mobile phone records revealed more damming evidence against Joe.

They showed he had been in contact with Nikki Pelley, the woman he claimed he was no longer having a relationship with.

Using the records from 4 October, Detective Garda Joanne O'Sullivan had put together a spreadsheet based on all of the outgoing and incoming calls and texts to Joe's phone.

It showed how Nikki's landline was used to ring Joe's mobile at 5.45am as he drove from his home to the gym. The call lasted 27 minutes and 43 seconds. Another call was made from Joe's mobile back to Nikki's landline at 7.35am. And a third call, this time from Nikki's mobile to Joe's mobile, was made at 8.12am and lasted for 25 minutes and 57 seconds.

The lovers were in contact more than eighteen times on the day of the murder.

The spreadsheet also illustrated how calls were made from Joe's mobile to Rachel's at 1.20pm, 1.26pm and 1.47pm. His phone also rang the house phone at 1.21pm and 1.50pm.

But what made this evidence so pertinent was the fact that Joe had admitted in interviews with the gardaí that he had his phone with him at all times on the day his wife was bludgeoned to death.

Detective Garda John Clancy also testified how gardaí were satisfied there was no possibility that Joe's phone could have been cloned by somebody else.

'As I understand it, the SIM card cannot be copied because of the number of digits on it. It is more complex, and it cannot be cloned,' he explained.

During a search of Joe's mother's house in Dunleer weeks after the murder, the gardaí had found a Nokia handset and the phone's IMEI number, a unique identification number, which matched the IMEI number of the mobile used by Joe on the day of the murder.

Although the evidence could not prove he had killed his wife, it had certainly established that he had lied about his movements.

The court heard that while interviewing Joe during his second arrest, Detective Garda Malachy Dunne quizzed him about his innocence.

'At no stage have you said you didn't kill Rachel. Can you look into my eyes and say you didn't kill Rachel?' he asked.

The detective's memo of that interview stated, 'Joe O'Reilly then looked into my eyes and said: "I did not kill Rachel."'

Dunne pressed Joe further: 'Do you deny you killed Rachel?' he asked.

'Yes,' replied Joe.

CHAPTER 8

Joe's Lies and Alibis

IT WAS NEARING the end of the third week of evidence, and the strain of the murder trial was beginning to visibly takes its toll on all concerned.

Day after day, the Callaly family sat on the same bench, in the same spots, listening intently to every single piece of evidence. Most days Rachel's father, Jimmy, who had noticeably aged in the 34 months since his daughter's death, just bowed his head, rarely looking up to see who was being questioned, patiently waiting for it all to be over.

Holding tightly to her husband's hand, his wife Rose held her head high, occasionally shifting her unflinching gaze from whoever was in the witness box to where her son-in-law sat.

Her children, Declan, Paul, Anne and Anthony, sat on either side of her, often linking arms or holding hands for much-needed support during the more distressing pieces of evidence.

On the thirteenth day of the trial, all of their reserves of strength were needed as they finally heard the full and shocking extent of Joe's aversion to his wife and the mother of his two boys.

A computer network engineer with Viacom, Roy Montgomery, explained to the court how he copied the details of Joe's email account, which was connected to the company's server, onto a CD and handed it over to the gardaí.

Detective Sergeant Gerard Keane then examined the CD, which showed a record of all the emails sent and received by Joe.

There were approximately 9,000. He found a series of five correspondences that had been sent and received on 9 June 2004 between Joe and his sister Ann, less than four months before Rachel's death.

Dominic McGinn read out the emails, which ran for almost 2,000 words. There was utter silence as Joe's vile expressions for his wife echoed around the courtroom and Rose, who had displayed such an extraordinary level of bravery and self-control, finally broke down.

The emails showed how Joe was afraid he would lose custody of his children if he divorced. One mail read as follows:

From: Ann O'Reilly
To: Joe O'Reilly
10.16am June 09, 2004

Hiya,

I'm just asking how you got on yesterday. How are you?

Concerned Banana.

Wanted to leave you alone yesterday to get your head together, but trust me, I held back on calling or mailing you. Let me know how things are and if you need anything.

From: Joe O'Reilly
To: Ann O'Reilly
10.41am June 09, 2004

In a nutshell, it was a big steaming pile of sh1te. They told us both, that shouting at the kids was okay, "sure we all do it".

Hitting kids is okay in the eyes of the law, as again "we all do it".

They never come out and visit the homes of kids reported as being abused unless the allegation is of a sexual nature or after several cases of non accidental hospitalisations.

Could it have gone any worse??? Yes!!!

Rachel is a "good mother" because she admits to having problems dealing with the kids and confessed to shouting at them on a daily basis. There is some Mickey Mouse course run once a year, to help parents cope with "difficult kids" and "parenting difficulties", and Rachel has volunteered to go on one. She was also playing the "home help" card but didn't get anywhere.

The best I got was a commitment to getting the district nurse pay a visit, as Adam is due his developmental check-up. Should have got it last year, but in the words of his mother: "You know yourself, what with the house move and so on, it's easy to forget these things."

Anyway, I gave them the go-ahead to drop out whenever they want to see the kids. Hopefully the DN will see her at her "best" or else the state of the house that the lazy c*nt leaves it, etc. . . .

Positives? Very few. At least it's on record that I don't need to attend the courses, I've no issues in dealing with the kids, and the complaint had nothing to do with me.

To answer your question as to how I am. Well, to be honest, I wasn't expecting much, as you were no doubt aware, so I wasn't too shocked with the apathy displayed by our wonderful child protection people.

That said, I think matters may get worse, as she told me in the car park that "I knew you were over-reacting going on to me about shouting at the kids. Did you hear them? Everybody does it, and I am a good mother."

Instead of giving her a slap on the wrist, it appears that they've forgiven her and patted her on the back for a job well done.

Did you get to talk to Derek by the way? Had to physically restrain him on Saturday night, not good. He's too much of a hot-head, but that said, you really couldn't blame him.

Adam was "reefed" up by the arm and dragged to bed, and she nearly tore Luke's ears off putting his PJ top on over his head. As usual, I had a right go at her, but as usual, by that stage the damage is already done.

Shouldn't really complain though, she is a "Wonderful Mother" in the eyes of the state.

Joe

PS. Interesting choice of terminology used by the Social Worker, everything was "Rachel is the main care giver and I was the secondary care giver."

I'm already "Mr Weekend Custody" in the eyes of the state. Doesn't bode too well does it? Oh, nearly forgot, the case is now closed to their satisfaction.

From: Ann O'Reilly
To: Joe O'Reilly
11.01am June 9, 2004

Well, at least you get the DN [District Nurse] coming out on unexpected visits, that can't be too bad really.

Dan was talking to her yesterday and she told him she now counts to ten and examines the situation with the kids, so let's hope something good, even if it's little, will come out of this.

So you're going out for a meal on Friday night with her. Should be good fun, all nice and romantic (not). Try again to talk to her about her lack of motherly instincts. Have you told her she's none? Does she admit to it?

Try a bit harder to talk to her about it. Tell her everything, be open and honest. I know I'd keep on trying constantly. I wouldn't give her ears a break from the subject. Otherwise she's just going to keep on living in cloud cuckoo land.

Did Derek say anything to Rachel about her manhandling Adam and Luke?

Ma was very worried about yesterday. If you get a minute could you ring her, put her mind at rest? I went straight into Ma's yesterday to see what the story was and she was saying that Rachel came in and was all over Adam and just blanked Luke (fooking bitch).

That hurt Ma, she wanted so much to say something but didn't. Anyway, Rachel stayed for chips, eggs and bread and was very calm and happy so Ma was left thinking.

Call her. She's our mammy and does really worry about us.

Don't let on that I told you, you know what she's like!

So do I still have to be on my best around Rachel keeping my mouth shut? If I see her hit or manhandle the kids can I speak up?

From Joe O'Reilly
To: Ann O'Reilly
3.42pm June 9, 2004

Hiya,

So she now counts to ten, eh? Believe that and you're not my sister!!!

Where the hell did you hear I was going for a night out with that c*nt???? A meal? I'd rather choke. Absolutely no way, never, not happening.

To quote your good self Ann, never look back, only look forward, eh?

Just to drill the point home, Me + Rachel + Marriage = over!!!!

I keep telling her, straight as you like, exactly what I think of her mothering instincts. Yes. In fact, to be even a little fair, I'm very aware that I'm over-critical at times, although I don't feel guilty about it to be honest, as she repulses me.

Derek didn't say anything, I wouldn't let him. Bad enough I have to bite my tongue and restrain myself, don't need him losing it. Not for her sake, but the kids wouldn't like seeing their mother abused by their uncle Derek, and I don't want his halo around them diminished in any way.

(You're getting competition Ann!!)

That's where you need to be careful. When Ma reported the incident, that brought about yesterday's farce, it very nearly came out as to who did the reporting!!!

The Suspect

You are prime suspect number one, you know it.
By all means, drag her fat ass outside and kick it into the
middle of next week, but not in front of the boys, and
don't leave any marks that can and will be used against
you in a court of law....

As I've said repeatedly, there is no talking to her.
She doesn't listen. Mind you there's a lot of that about.
I told you and I told Ma that this would amount to
nothing, and you both knew better than me and went
through the usual series of questions.

I'm not having a go Ann, but it really wound me up
last time, as I go through every angle I can with the boys
before I make a move.

Yesterday proved yet again, the injustices that exist
in this country.

As a mother, you can shout and scream and smack
almost as much as you want to, once you admit to
having a bit of a problem and then volunteer to a lip
service parent's course.

Maybe now, you'll both listen to what I have to say
and not go about with your heads in the sand.

Being a father in this country, no matter how good,
will land you with weekend visitations and not much
else. You know of one case where full custody was
given, that's great, and good for him. I know of dozens
where it went the other way.

Yesterday was my first personal indication of how
much I will lose if I don't try different angles. After all,
I'm only the secondary care giver...

I do appreciate your support; and I know the
boys mean the world to you, they are my life and I am
nothing without them.

Adam was the one singled out as the child whom the concerns were about. More bad news for Luke as proved yesterday, in your own words and observations.

Ann, there is only so much crap the kid can deal with and patients [sic] are running on empty. You saw first hand the number she did on him before.

I'd rather die than see him go through that again. He won't go through that again, end of story.

Be as good as you can around Rachel for now, but tell me everything you see, do not hold back.

If you see her being excessive, then step in. I want to know as much as possible, and I can't be there all the time. Ann, you're my sister, my blood, she's not. What you tell me, will not be questioned. You have carte blanche visitation rights to my house, and to my kids. In fact the more you're around, the better. Same with Dan, but I don't want him knowing too much.

I plan on calling Ma later tonight. I know she's worried, but I couldn't call last night, as I didn't know if she had a visitor and her family. The "World's Greatest Mum" is out tonight, getting laid with a bit of luck, so I'll have time to talk to Ma properly when the boys are asleep.

I'll be home in Ma's on Friday with the boys, so I'll see you then?

Thanks for the concern, sorry for the long email!!

Joe

> From: Ann O'Reilly
> To: Joe O'Reilly
> 4pm June 9, 2004

Your meal is probably a surprise. Well of course it is.

She got Dan to book it last night for ye then you are staying in Ma's but she asked me last week if she ever wanted to venture up to Dunleer and eat out could she stay with me???

So she knows the marriage is over then and it's a divorce. What does she say to that? Maybe that's why she's taking you out on Friday. Say nothing...

I do get it now. Your fooked as a father in this dump. Ask her to move abroad. I really dunno how you're going to get out of this one.

So when are you filing for legal separation then?

If you want I can kidnap you and the kids on Friday night before she has chance to get hold of you. We could go on a trip in my car??

Or you could just go with her and ignore her the whole night or stare at sexy ladies.

This was the first time the court had fully heard about how Rachel had been reported to the authorities for being rough with her children.

Judging by the Callalys' reaction when it was read out in court that Joe's mother Ann had been the one to report Rachel, it was clear their long-term suspicions had been finally confirmed.

At the back of the room Ann O'Reilly had closed her eyes briefly and bowed her head while the emails that had passed between her son and daughter were read out.

The evidence was the last piece of business that day. As friends and family of the Callalys rushed over to comfort them, Joe left through a side door, successfully avoiding crossing the path of his in-laws.

The following morning Nikki Pelley finally took the stand.

Onlookers craned their necks to get a look at her as she made her way through the crowded room. She swiftly made her way to the witness box, refusing to catch anyone's eye and carefully avoiding even turning her head in the direction of Joe. Far from being a gibbering mess or visibly distressed to be giving evidence in her lover's murder trial, she held herself well. In fact there was almost an air of defiance about her.

Under the intense scrutiny of the tense courtroom, she began her evidence by confirming that she lived at her parents' home in Rathfarnham. Her testimony rarely strayed from short, measured answers.

She then explained how her affair with Joe had begun and confirmed they started to sleep together three or four times a week. She claimed Joe had told her his marriage to Rachel had been effectively over for about a year before she met him. And that 'they had separate bedrooms'.

Nikki said she had never met Rachel, although she did see her once at a softball event, and as far as she knew, Rachel had no idea that she was sleeping with Joe. But she did know that Joe used to tell Rachel he was staying over at his office when in fact he was staying at her place.

'Why did he say the office?' one of the prosecution team asked.

'He didn't say,' she replied.

The two also went down to Nikki's family's holiday home in Wexford for a couple of days, but she could not remember the excuse he gave to Rachel for the trip.

And she told the court how she had met the O'Reilly's two little boys, Luke and Adam 'on a number of occasions on Saturday afternoons, either at home or at the zoo.'

Joe had introduced them to her as 'Nikki . . . just Nikki.'

Much to the visible distress of the Callaly family, she admitted that she had stayed over on one occasion at the O'Reilly's home, but when asked where Rachel was at the time she replied, 'I can't remember. I think down the country somewhere. I don't know.'

She was then quizzed about her contact with Joe on the day of the murder. She admitted to talking to him on the phone at 10.30pm on the night before the killing but claimed he had mentioned nothing in particular.

And she said she had rung Joe at around 5.45am the following morning but claimed the conversation had not been very long, 'maybe 15 to 20 minutes'.

But when it was put to her that the phone call had been 27 minutes, as the phone evidence had already revealed, she said it 'possibly' could have been. And she said she was not able to remember phoning him back at 8.12am, though the phone records indicated she had.

She was then brought through the interviews she had with the gardaí on the 5 and 27 October in 2004. When questioned about her relationship with Joe she told them 'it was just an affair'.

'Why did you tell them that,' asked the prosecution.

'I don't know. I just did,' she replied.

Initially she claimed that it was she who had decided to play down her relationship with Joe. But later, in the absence of the jury, the statement she had given to the gardaí on 16 November 2004 was read back to her.

She had told officers that it was Joe who had told her not to let on that they had been seeing each other to the extent they had been. And she told them that this discussion had taken place on the day after Rachel's murder.

The trial judge reminded her of the seriousness of the oath she had taken earlier that morning, and later when asked the same question again, but this time in front of the jury, she replied, 'Joe had told me that's what he said [about the affair] and I should say the same.'

She also acknowledged the reason as to why Joe had made this suggestion.

'Because if it was a relationship it would be seen as giving him a motive to kill Rachel,' she rather reluctantly explained.

She then revealed that the pair had discussed their future and had talked about being permanently together. 'There were two options with the children,' Nikki explained. 'Either staying with Joe or staying with Rachel. He would have preferred full custody, but he would have settled for joint custody.'

The prosecution then presented two halves of two separate credit cards to the court. They were handed to Nikki and she was asked to put them together and read out the name that it made.

'Ms Nikki P Reilly,' she said.

'Who did that?' asked the prosecution.

'Either myself or Joe . . . for fun, it was a joke. They were two old visa cards,' she explained.

The prosecution moved on.

'What name did Mr O'Reilly use for addressing his wife?' he asked.

'Normally Rach or Rachel,' said Nikki. But the prosecution pressed on.

'Any others?'

Nikki told the court that if the O'Reilly's were arguing, Joe would call Rachel a 'wasp' or a 'cunt,' but she claimed it wasn't a term he used often.

She explained she was aware of some of the arguments the couple had and described them as 'routine, run-of-the-mill' rows.

According to her evidence, she became aware of Rachel's death on the day of the murder approximately between 3.15pm and 3.30pm.

'I rang Joe,' she explained.

'He said to me that Rachel was dead, that he was with the police and he said, "I will talk to you later."'

The prosecution then jumped forward to the night of 22 October, when Joe and Rose Callaly had appeared on the *Late Late Show* to make an appeal for anyone with any information about Rachel's murder to come forward.

'Where did Mr O'Reilly stay that night?' Vaughan-Buckley asked.

'He stayed in my house,' she replied.

'Did he stay overnight?'

'He did, that's correct,' she replied. Her testimony over, she then quickly left the courtroom.

Detective Sergeant Michael Gubbins told how he had retrieved a number of text messages from Joe to Nikki's Nokia phone that she had saved.

Seven of these were read out by McGinn, a member of the prosecution team. In the texts, Joe referred to Adam and Luke as belonging to Nikki and himself.

10.02pm July 16, 2004
Hey, I will only be your husband. I know my place.

8.29am July 17, 2004
Good morning beautiful. I am completely crazy about you and can't wait to see you later.

11.51pm July 27, 2004
Sweet dreams too love. I can't ever begin to tell you how much I both miss you and love you. You are everything to me. XXX

12.37pm August 8, 2004
Just to text you. Our boy had his first school day. He had fun but will have lots of homework tomorrow. Love you. XXX.

10.33pm September 15, 2004
Ditto. My beautiful bride to be.
10.09pm September 30, 2004
All your willies tucked up in bed. Lights out and missing you. Sweet dreams my darling. I love you.

7.10pm October 1, 2004
You are meant to remind me?!! Okay, I understand. All
the boys down on the beach, only thing missing is you.
XXX.

It had also emerged that Nikki was not the first
woman Joe had had an affair with.

In 2003, when his youngest son was not even two
years old, he had a relationship with a woman from
Limerick. He would tell Rachel that he had to go
on 'overnighters' for the company. The relationship
lasted only a few months and had 'fizzled out' by the
summer of 2003.

When the woman discovered Joe was actually
married, he told her that he was effectively separated
from his wife but was concerned about losing access to
his children. In fact he told the woman that he would
not even 'tolerate' joint custody.

It was a disclosure the prosecution in the murder
trial hoped to use as proof of Joe's motive to kill Rachel.
The judge, however, ruled the woman's testimony
inadmissible as their relationship had broken up well
over a year before Rachel's death.

Justice White said it was too lengthy a period of
time to be relevant: 'It seems to me its prejudicial value
outweighs its probative value.'

The garda telecommunications section had also
collected the voicemails left on Rachel's mobile and
landline phones on the day of the murder.

The first had been left by Joe who claimed that
he had assumed Rachel had called over to her friend

Jackie Connor's house that morning to wish her a happy birthday. These were also read out to the court.

From Joe O'Reilly.
11.52am:
How're you doing? Just 12 o'clock. Just ringing to see where you are. Obviously you're at Jackie's chewing the fat and not listening to messages from me.

Give us a shout. Let me know where you are and how your morning is, the usual sort of stuff. Okay. Good luck and don't forget to wish Jackie's a happy birthday for me.

Okay. Goodbye.

Another message left by Helen Moore of Tots United was read out.

From Helen Moore of Tots United Montessori crèche.
12.50pm:
Helen here. Just approaching five to one. Just giving you a ring to see are you on your way and is everything okay?

Alright talk to you soon.

After she failed to contact Rachel, she rang Joe, who then rang his wife back a couple of times.

From Joe O'Reilly.
1.18pm:
Hi Rach, it's only me. I just got a call from Helen in the Montessori. You have not picked up Adam. Was Sarah meant to pick him up or something?

You have no doubt left your mobile at home or in the back of the car or something.

Helen has to go and pick up her own kids. She'll be back at 1.50pm.

Don't panic if you get there and she is not there. I'm on the way anyway, just in case.

I'm going to use the house number.

Okay. Thank you, bye.

From Joe O'Reilly
1.24pm:
Rach, it's Joe, I've tried your number I don't know how many times now and you're not answering.

You're not in Jackie's or at your mother. I am now really, really worried about you. Will you please call me?

This is not funny. It's not like you. I am actually worried. Please ring me.

At this stage, Rachel's mother was now trying to get in touch with him to find out why she had not collected Adam.

From Rose Callaly
1.33pm:
Rach, its Mam ringing here. It's twenty to two. Will you ring me as soon as possible please?

On his way driving towards their home, Joe rang Rachel's phone again.

From Joe O'Reilly
1.45pm:
    Rach, it's me again. I'm just coming onto the M1 from the M50 now. I have just spoken to your mother. She is going to pop on out. Please ring me.
    I've been crying. You have me worried. If you . . . I don't know. Talk to me please.

Gardaí also retrieved a text that Joe had sent to Rachel at 10.07am which read:

You and the boys sleep okay? Wish Jackie a happy birthday for me. XXX

Joe had admitted in interviews with the gardaí that he had his phone with him at all times throughout the day of the murder. The court was again told that Joe had been arrested and interviewed on 17 November 2004 and 14 March 2006.

During the first arrest, Joe was asked what must have seemed like a totally innocuous question by a detective sergeant—did he have his mobile phone with him throughout the day of the murder.

'Yes, I think so,' Joe had replied.

He was asked the question another way: 'And you had your phone with you when you answered it?'

Joe replied, 'Yes.'

The strangest evidence heard that day, however, was the voice message left on Rachel's mobile phone by Joe at 8.24am on 4 November 2004, exactly a month after the murder.

'Hi Rachy, it's Joe. I am really, really sorry for the very early phone call,' it said.

'This time exactly a month ago you were probably doing what I am doing now, getting the kids ready for school. Now you are so cold.

'The sun was out. It was a normal day. You had less than two hours to live. Sorry, I just want to go back in time and say I love you, but I can't.

'Goodbye. I miss you. I don't want to live without you. That's the truth. Sleep well. Rest in peace. I have got to go and get the boys into the car now. But first I want to get them dressed for school.

'Good morning sweetheart. I miss you and I love you. Chat to you later, Goodbye.'

By this stage, the prosecution had ruled out all of the people Joe had claimed could have had a grudge against him or Rachel. But the court had yet to hear from a young man called Wesley Kearns, whom Joe had fired.

The witness explained how he had worked at the company as a billposter for nearly two years before Joe started there. And that after about a month of his joining, Joe 'started to throw his weight around and took contracts off a lot of people'. He said Joe gave out to him, claiming he hadn't put a poster up when he said he had.

'The day he fired you, you threw a fire extinguisher at him and he locked himself in his office?' asked Vaughan-Buckley.

Wesley confirmed this incident and added that until then his relationship with Joe had been good.

'I did like him, yeah, up until he sacked me,' he said to the stifled giggles of the courtroom.

His alibi for the day of the murder was that he was at the Labour Exchange in Clondalkin, where he stayed between 9am and midday. He was never a suspect, but the prosecution were forced to ask the question for the benefit of the jury.

Detective Garda Sean Fitzpatrick had spent weeks going through the 119 separate pieces of CCTV footage that were seized by the gardaí as part of their investigation into Rachel's death. The video tapes and CDs came from various premises around north Dublin, the city and areas around Joe's workplace at Bluebell, including petrol stations, shop car-parks and the front reception of Joe's office.

He compiled a comprehensive report of sightings of cars that were similar to Joe's Fiat Marea, a navy blue estate car.

In an almost forty minute presentation, he showed the court his findings on the two large plasma television screens both mounted on the walls on either side of the judge's bench.

The jury was brought through the journey the gardaí believed Joe made that morning, from his workplace to his home in Naul and then back down again into the north of the city, a trip which took place at the time Joe had told gardaí he was at Broadstone inspecting buses.

The footage was by no means conclusive, for the best part blurry and at no time capturing a licence plate number that could definitely identify the car as his.

The most that could be said about the sightings was that they showed a dark, estate-type car similar to a Fiat Marea.

The footage from the reception area at Viacom in Bluebell, however, clearly showed Joe leaving the building at 8.07am. And another camera caught a car fitting the description of Joe's leaving the industrial estate at 8.12am.

The detective then showed footage from the Europrise premises at Blake's Cross in north Dublin.

'At 8.55:49am I observed what I believe to be a navy coloured estate car travelling north [in the direction of the O'Reilly home],' he explained.

The next sighting of interest was from a camera covering the entrance and part of the roadway outside of Murphy's Quarry, which is 850 metres from the O'Reilly home.

'At 9.03:30am I observed what I believe to be Rachel O'Reilly's Renault Scenic passing the quarry, travelling south, away from the house,' the detective said.

This made sense as it was around the time that Rachel dropped off the two boys at crèche and school.

'At 9.10:32am I observed what I believe to be a navy coloured estate car passing by the quarry heading in the direction of the house,' the officer continued.

'At 9.41:29am I observed a vehicle heading in the direction of O'Reilly household, which I believe to be Rachel O'Reilly's Renault Scenic. Eighteen minutes later at 9.59:22am I observed what I believe to be a navy-coloured estate car pass the quarry from the direction of the O'Reilly house going south.'

The next sighting of a navy-coloured estate car was on the CCTV camera at Blake's Cross.

'At 10.07:02am a navy-coloured estate car similar to a Fiat Marea travelling south,' the detective continued.

He went on to explain that later that day at 2.14pm, around the time Joe was arriving home after collecting Adam from crèche, a similar navy-coloured estate car was seen passing Murphy's Quarry in the direction of the O'Reilly household again.

The prosecuting team set about comparing the navy estate car sightings with the location of Joe's mobile phone that morning, which had previously been detailed in court.

The jury was reminded that at 9.25am, a call was placed from Quearney's phone to Joe's mobile. It showed that Joe's phone was in the area near Murphy's Quarry at the time, while Quearney was in the Broadstone area.

Then there was a text sent to Joe at 9.52am by his friend Kieran Gallagher that also placed the phone in the vicinity of the base station at Murphy's Quarry.

And there was the sighting of a navy blue estate passing Blake's Cross at 10.07am.

A text was sent from Joe's phone to his wife just 28 seconds later and that communication was routed through the Richardstown station, which serves the Blake's Cross area.

Fitzpatrick had also examined CCTV footage from the Broadstone bus depot and Church Street on the north of the city.

'I observed Derek Quearney arriving at the reception area of Broadstone at 9.26:31am,' he said.

When he was asked if he saw Joe on that CCTV footage, he said no.

He told how he had studied footage on Church Street, a route used to get to Broadstone.

'Did you at any stage see a car similar to Mr O'Reilly's navy Fiat Marea driving up Church Street in the direction of Broadstone,' he was asked.

He had not seen such a car, but he did spot a vehicle that he believed to be Quearney's Citroen Xsara passing up Church Street in the direction of Broadstone at 9.19am.

Later that morning, at 11.10am, the detective said he observed what be believed to be Quearney's car driving back down Church Street.

'I believe it to be his car because that was missing a hubcap. Moving directly behind that was a car which I believe was a Fiat Marea,' he said.

Joe and Quearney could later be seen returning to Viacom's office within seconds of each other at 11.48am.

Detective Garda Jim McGovern then explained that he had reconstructed a journey from Murphy's Quarry to the Broadstone depot on 8 November 2004. Using the speaking clock as his gauge, he testified that it took around 40 minutes in 'generally normal traffic.'

Gardaí had sent the footage to a forensic imagery analyst in the UK.

Andrew Laws was hired to give evidence in such cases and gave a robust and confident appearance.

He explained how 'CCTV imagery is generally poorer than the public's perception of it.'

He detailed the three tests he and his colleagues carried out when studying such footage for comparative purposes. The first test compares the general measurements of the cars in the different pieces of footage to see if they were the same or different.

The second test compared specific features on both cars for likenesses or differences, and the third uses video technology to superimpose one car on another to check for similarities. Laws pointed out the limitations of the process several times and admitted that he and others in the same line of business 'could not be conclusive in our conclusions.'

He explained his findings could be put into context by placing them on a scale of possible findings. The scale starts at the bottom with 'no support' and goes upwards through 'limited support,' 'moderate support,' 'support,' 'strong support,' and all the way up to 'powerful support'.

In the end he told the court that after his analysis he could not rule out the possibility that a car seen on the Murphy's Quarry footage on the day of her murder was Joe's and he concluded there was 'moderate support' for the belief that a car seen passing the quarry was the same make and model as Joe's navy blue Fiat Marea estate.

He also found there was 'strong support' for the belief that a car seen passing near Blake's Cross, which is eight kilometres south of the O'Reilly home, was the same make.

Laws was the final witness out of 144 called by the prosecution.

It was now the turn of the defence who began by calling Joe's work colleague, Derek Quearney.

Throughout the trial his name had been used repeatedly but this was the first time anyone had even gotten a glimpse of the former soldier.

A rather short man with wire-rimmed glasses, he emerged from the crowd at the back of the courtroom and made his way to the witness box.

He took a swift look to his left to where Joe was sitting before taking the stand. Earlier the court had been told how Joe had described his friendship with Quearney as a close working relationship and claimed they had little to do with each other outside work issues.

Gageby began his questioning by asking him about his background. In his strong yet articulate Dublin accent, Quearney explained that he had been brought up in Ballyfermot but now lived in Kildare.

He told the court he was 46, had spent 21 years in the army, and after leaving in 1998, joined an advertising agency called TDI, which was later taken over by Viacom.

Quearney was then asked by Gageby to bring the court through the morning of the murder.

He said he met Joe in his office at 8am and they arranged to do an inspection of Damian Tully's work, who had been instructed to place advertisements on the side of buses at the Broadstone bus depot in Phibsborough.

'Joe went ahead. I had to stay behind to issue instructions to the various drivers. I left at about nine o'clock, ten to nine, something like that,' Quearney explained and said that he arrived at the depot in his silver Citroen Xsara at around 9.30am.

'Once I got to Broadstone bus depot, I parked my car. I then rang Joe to see where he was. He said he was at the back of the pits,' Quearney continued.

'I got out of my car and said I'd see him there and I walked over towards the main Broadstone building.

'I told the foreman I was there. When any member of Viacom goes to the depot they are supposed to tell the foreman before they do a bus inspection. I inspected four or five buses in the pits. After that I met with Joe at the back of the pits, maybe 15 or 20 minutes later.'

Quearney said this happened between 9.50am and 10am and that they then 'went around and inspected all the buses in the Phibsborough yard.'

It was explained that the bus depot complex is split into two separate sections, the Broadstone and Phibsborough yards.

'Joe stayed back [in the Phibsborough yard],' Quearney said. 'I went down to Broadstone to see any other buses.' He said the inspections continued until 10.30am, when he met Joe again.

'Some more buses had come in to Phibsborough,' he said. 'We inspected the rest of the buses that were down there and walked towards the entrance. We finished off the inspection and headed off around 11am. I was driving my Citroen Xsara and Joe was driving his Fiat Marea. I went out first. As I got to the exit of the depot I was going towards Constitution Hill and a bus stopped to let me out. Joe was right behind me at that time.'

Quearney then told how he met with gardaí at his office on the night of the murder and made a statement describing Joe's movements earlier that day. He made a follow-up statement two days later.

He told the court he was shocked when on 16 November, he was arrested on suspicion of withholding information by gardaí who had earlier asked him to meet them at the Sheldon Park Hotel in Ballyfermot. He was detained and questioned at Balbriggan Garda Station in Louth for around 40 hours before being released without charge.

'[I was in] absolute shock. I just couldn't believe that I was being arrested,' he said.

'The gardaí went through my statements and were expressing that I must be wrong on my timing. They then showed me phone evidence. They told me they were the phone calls I had made to Joe and were asking me if I could be wrong. I then conceded at that stage that I could have been wrong in my timing.'

According to Quearney, the gardaí told him there was a 30 to 40 minute time gap between his account of Joe's movements and the account given by the phone records.

'I conceded it was possible [I was wrong], but that is not the way I remember it,' he said.

The court was told that gardaí met Quearney again in March 2006 and showed him a presentation tracking the movement of Joe's phone on the day of the murder.

'Again I thought, I have said it is very possible I am wrong. I just can't explain the lapse of 30-40 minutes,' he said.

'That is the way on the day I remember the inspection.'

Quearney was asked again what time he thought he met Joe at Broadstone on the morning of the murder. He replied: 'I think it was 9.50am or 10am.'

But when questioned by the prosecuting counsel, Vaughan-Buckley, Quearney said the earliest he could definitely say he saw Joe at Broadstone was at around 11am.

'It was pointed out to you that your evidence was not correct as Joe O'Reilly's mobile phone was in north Co Dublin at the time,' said the prosecutor.

'I said at the time and I am saying now, it is possible my timing was wrong,' Quearney replied.

'It is possible, but it is not the way I remember it.'

The prosecuting counsel then read from a statement Quearney made to gardaí on 2 March 2006, in which he confirmed he had been shown O_2 mobile phone reports concerning Joe's mobile phone on the day of the murder and a presentation of those movements.

'From these reports, I accept my original timing of seeing Joe O'Reilly at Broadstone Bus Depot on 4 October could be wrong,' his statement read.

'I wish to add the only time I can be definitely sure about seeing Mr O'Reilly was at the time I rang [his work colleague] Noel Paget's mobile phone.

'I accept the time of the phone-call was 10.59am on 4 October. That was at the very end of the inspection.'

Vaughan-Buckley asked Quearney about the 9.25am call made by him to Joe, which was picked up by the Murphy's Quarry base station and lasted two minutes and seven seconds.

'What was the call about?'

Quearney said, 'I asked Joe, "Where are you?" He told me he was at the back of the pits at Broadstone bus depot.'

The witness was once again asked if he stood over the original time he gave to the gardaí for meeting Joe at Broadstone.

'I accept I am possibly wrong as I've said all along, but that is not my recollection of that day,' he replied.

Quearney had simply been mistaken in his timing.

Quearney then told the court that he was aware of Joe's affair with Nikki Pelley. He was asked what Joe had told him to do if anyone queried where he was when he was with Nikki.

'He told me if he was going out for the affair and if anyone rang, to say he was out of the office,' he explained.

'Did you and Mr O'Reilly cover for each other at the office,' asked Vaughan-Buckley.

'He'd cover if I headed off early and stuff like that,' replied Quearney.

He was then questioned by the defence.

'Would you ever cover for anyone who murdered?' Gageby asked.

'Absolutely not,' was the fervent reply.

The defence had just one more witness, a former schoolmate of Joe's who had read about the case in the papers and decided to come forward as a witness.

Joseph O'Shea explained how he had been two years ahead of Joe at Greendale Community School in Kilbarrack.

He had read that Joe was claiming he was at Broadstone at the time of the murder. The glazer said a 'light bulb went off' in his head as he remembered seeing Joe outside Broadstone at some stage. And after discussing it with his wife and work colleagues, he decided to approach gardaí on 11 July.

In his statement, however, O'Shea admitted he could not remember what date or time he saw Joe. All he could say for certain was that it was lashing rain on the morning he drove past Broadstone and had spotted his old schoolmate.

The prosecution counsel reminded the jury that they had heard evidence from a weather expert who testified it had been sunny throughout Dublin on the day of the murder.

The trial judge, Justice White, intervened in this part of the trial and asked O'Shea if he remembered how Joe had been dressed.

'No,' he replied.

'Did he have any rain gear?' asked the judge.

'I just know I seen him,' said O'Shea.

The last witness had given his evidence. All that remained were the closing addresses from the prosecution, the defence and the Judge.

After that it would be finally time for the jury of nine men and two women to consider and come to a verdict.

CHAPTER 9

'Justice, Thank God, Justice'

AFTER 19 DAYS of evidence, the end of this extraordinary murder trial was finally within sight.

Word had spread that it was nearly all over and the crowds coming down to catch a glimpse of the proceedings had swelled to never-before seen proportions at the Four Courts. Long-time employees at the courts told how the numbers arriving down each morning, hours before the hearings even started, were larger than those seen at the infamous Catherine Nevin trial a few years previously.

Wearing the same sharp black suit he had worn throughout the trial, Joe sat in his place waiting for the barristers to begin. For the first time he looked noticeably tired, his face was pale and there were dark circles under his eyes. D-Day was fast approaching.

At approximately 11.20am, the prosecutor Dominic McGinn began his powerful, lengthy and detailed monologue. He began by acknowledging the enormous amount of evidence the jury had to absorb and promised to 'attempt to bring it into focus'.

For the next two hours he outlined the reasons that he believed would persuade the jury to find Joe guilty. And while admitting all the evidence against Joe was circumstantial, he claimed when put together they would prove the father-of-two's guilt 'beyond a reasonable doubt'.

Using the well-respected analogy often quoted in cases where a verdict relies on circumstantial evidence, he described the various bits of evidence as being like the strands of a rope.

'The individual strands might not be strong enough, but when you tie them all together, they are,' he explained.

He took the jury through the CCTV evidence that showed Rachel's car returning home after dropping off her kids to school and he said it was clear the attack had happened almost immediately after she got back to the house, as her car keys were found under her body.

He returned to the distressing evidence of the violent nature of Rachel's death presented by the forensic experts, Dr Marie Cassidy and Dr Diane Daly. And he explained how the gardaí had quickly ruled out their initial theory that she had been killed by a burglar.

There was so much blood that a fleeing intruder would have been covered in it or at least would have left a trail behind him either inside or outside the house, but none was found anywhere else. McGinn said this showed that whoever killed Rachel 'didn't panic' and 'took his time' afterwards to wash the blood off himself before leaving. It was also significant that a lot of cash had been left behind. There were €450 in a handbag and €860 in a container in the utility room, both of which would have been very easy to find.

But all that was taken from the house were a few insignificant items that were found in a ditch near the house, had no traces of blood on them and actually looked as though they had been placed there.

The barrister said there was nothing sinister about the discovery of blood on the washing machine that had been traced to Rachel's birth brother Thomas Lowe; he had simply 'cut himself doing carpentry work' a couple of months beforehand.

And he said anyone Joe claimed might have had a grudge against Rachel or himself had given solid accounts of where they were on the day of the murder.

He also pointed to Joe's affair with Nikki Pelley. 'This wasn't just extramarital sex,' said McGinn. 'They were planning to make a future and a home together.' He reminded them of the two halves of the Visa card that spelled out the name 'Ms Nikki P Reilly' and text messages Joe had sent her.

'The tone of the texts was very clear as regards Mr O'Reilly's feelings towards Ms Pelley,' he said.

And there were the emails Joe had sent his sister Ann, which made it clear how he felt about his wife in the months before her death and that he was worried about losing custody of his children.

'That's what his real state of mind was,' said McGinn. 'And that is motive, ladies and gentlemen.'

McGinn went on to dismantle Joe's alibi. He said the mobile phone evidence proved Joe was in the area of his home when Rachel was murdered.

'We know from the evidence that the same SIM card and the same handset were used throughout the period; therefore it can't be the case that somebody cloned his phone,' he said. 'And more importantly, he admitted to gardaí from the outset that he had his phone with him at all times.

'A mobile phone these days is like an extension of someone's hand,' he added. 'Common sense tells us that wherever the phone was, Mr O'Reilly was.'

Once again he brought them through the spreadsheet of calls and tests to and from Joe's phone that day, and he reminded them how a mobile phone expert testified it would have been impossible for a call received by Joe while he was at Broadstone to have been routed through a base station at Murphy's Quarry.

McGinn then moved on to Quearney's alibi for Joe where he claimed he had met the suspect at Broadstone between 9.50am and 10am.

He recounted how he admitted that he might have been mistaken about the time he met Joe that morning. And in the end the only time Quearney could say for certain that he saw Joe at the depot was at 10.59am when Joe was standing beside him as he phoned a work colleague.

'Perhaps Mr O'Reilly's alibi is not as watertight as it might have seemed. It was reliant on an unreliable witness,' said McGinn. 'Bear in mind Mr Quearney is somebody who worked with Mr O'Reilly for a number of years. Bear in mind that Mr Quearney would cover for Mr O'Reilly's affair. When Mr O'Reilly was with Ms Pelley, he said he would say he was somewhere else.'

And then there was the CCTV footage where the gardaí were unable to find any trace of Joe's car heading up Church Street in the direction of Broadstone that morning. Perhaps a lorry passed in front of the camera and O'Reilly was after having "bad luck," conceded McGinn.

But the barrister questioned if it was also 'bad luck' that a car similar to Joe's Fiat Marea estate was seen on two separate CCTV cameras close to his home that day.

'In all, five sightings of a similar car were picked up by cameras at Murphy's Quarry and Blake's Cross,' he said.

'At the same time those cars were seen, Mr O'Reilly's phone was found to have been in the general area,' he said. And what were the chances of a different estate car, similar to Joe's, being seen on the back roads of north Co. Dublin that day?

'Was that just all bad luck?' he asked the jury. 'Are all of these images on CCTV just a series of coincidences?'

They could not be, he insisted.

'The reality of the situation is that Mr O'Reilly was not at work and was not at Broadstone when his wife was killed. He was in north Co. Dublin in the coverage of the Murphy's Quarry mast.

'What this tells you is that Mr O'Reilly lied. He lied about his alibi.'

Summing it all up, he told the jury that Joe was the only person with a reason to kill Rachel.

'He is the only person with a motive,' said McGinn. 'The only rational explanation is that Mr O'Reilly killed his wife. Because of that, I suggest you can't have a reasonable doubt. If you have no reasonable doubt, then you must convict him.'

Gageby was next to speak. He was no less powerful or convincing.

Jumping to his feet, he spoke to the jury about the extremely serious nature of what they were being asked to do. The decision they made in this case would not be reversible, and whatever conclusion they came to would stand for all time, he warned.

He acknowledged that many people might not like Joe because he had an affair and had said nasty things about his wife.

'So he lets off steam, so he uses bad language [which is] really unpleasant. So what? Where is the homicide?' Gageby asked the jury.

He went on to accuse the defence of setting out to discredit Joe at every opportunity because he had an affair with Nikki Pelley. He said the prosecution's case had 'a lot of innuendo and allegation but only a little bit of substance'.

He told jurors, 'If the accused was not a man having an affair or being disloyal to his wife, it would be a lot easier to give him the benefit of the doubt. If he was incredibly likeable, did a lot of work for charity or had won medals for Ireland, you would approach this case differently. But this is not a court of morality; it is a court of law. You are now the judges. You are in the driving seat.'

Turning his attention to the immense amount of media coverage the case had attracted, he urged the jury not to reach the verdict he claimed the press wanted just because it would 'sell more newspapers'.

'In the past 40 to 50 years I don't think I've seen a case that has been accompanied each day by so many journalists and people who have queued up to get in,' he said.

'I always approach cases with the view that publicity is unwelcome because they try to skew things. You must reach a decision in this case without any consideration to the publicity.

'The more difficult thing to do is something which is unpopular. You have to examine your conscience and reach the right decision.'

Returning to the prosecution's case, Gageby questioned the motive they had presented for Joe to kill his wife.

'It's quite clear the marriage was not happy and my client was having an affair, but he's not the first person to have one and he won't be the last,' he said.

'There was no history of violence in the family and the man had never been in trouble before, but then out of the blue he decides to murder his wife?'

He asked the jurors how many of them had discussed a break-up with someone and 'not used nice terms'.

'We have a phrase in our business that the first casualty of a marital dispute is the truth,' he said.

'People use emotive language all the time, and people let off steam about their wives and partners. So what?'

He reminded the jury that the witness John Austin had told them Joe was planning to move out of his home to an apartment in Balbriggan so he could be close to his children.

'Is this the action of someone who is going to kill their wife,' asked Gageby. 'Yet in some way the prosecution was saying Mr O'Reilly decided, "I'll kill her to solve the custody situation."'

He also questioned why the gardaí had been so anxious to get Joe's alibi, Derek Quearney, to change his story if the phone records placing him at Murphy's Quarry were so reliable.

'If the phone evidence was the bee's knees, the big stumbling block of the case, why were the gardaí so anxious to get Derek Quearney to admit he could have been wrong about the time?' he asked.

And why had the gardaí been unable to find CCTV footage of Joe's Fiat Marea estate south of Blake's Cross.

'What comes up must come down,' he said, referring to the prosecution's belief that Joe drove up to his home to kill Rachel and then drove back south to the Broadstone bus depot.

If this was the case then why didn't the officers find any footage of Joe when he arrived back into the city and was moving towards the depot, Gageby demanded.

'There isn't a pinch of such evidence,' he said. 'They fall apart on that. How could a car like that evade CCTV. The simple answer is it couldn't have been on CCTV because it wasn't there.'

And he pointed out that if the prosecution was right in its calculations, Joe would have had only about 18 minutes to kill Rachel, take a shower to wash off the blood, put on a clothes wash and jump back in his car.

'From 9.41am to 9.59am,' he said. 'Everything has to be done in that [time] if the prosecution is right.' And he asked the jury why nobody had made an effort to re-enact the allegation; nobody had tried to spend the time at the house that it would have taken him to kill Rachel and 'come back down'.

The prosecution's case, he said, was based on a 'large amount of suspicion with a little bit of science'.

Gageby then dismissed the unusual things Joe had said to friends and family in the aftermath of Rachel's death, for instance when he told Helen Reddy that his wife had not been sexually assaulted before the post mortem was carried out.

He claimed that something like this was very easy to say over the phone to a distressed friend. And too much had been made out of the fact that Joe told another friend of Rachel's he believed the murder weapon was 'in the water'.

According to Gageby, this was a 'perfectly natural thing to say' given the extensive speculation about the case in the newspapers at the time.

His points made, the defence counsel sat down.

✤ ✤ ✤ ✤ ✤

The following morning Justice Barry White began his own summation. In his soft, yet clear and firm tone, the white-haired judge began by telling the nine men and two women that his instruction was final.

With a half-smile he said, 'I am like the Pope in matters of faith—infallible as far as you are concerned in matters of law.'

He explained that Joe was entitled to the presumption of innocence, that he did not have to prove that he had not murdered Rachel; rather it was up to the State to prove his guilt beyond a reasonable doubt.

The judge advised the jury to put themselves in Joe's position and ask themselves how they would feel if they were convicted on the basis of the evidence that had been heard. 'If you say, "Well no, I would not be happy to be convicted on that evidence, I would not feel that I had got justice," then the State has failed to satisfy you as to the guilt of the accused man.'

He also instructed them only to make their decision on the basis of the evidence they had heard in the court and nothing else, and that they should not assume anything about Joe just because he did not take the stand during the case.

'There is no onus on the accused to give evidence or to answer questions by the gardaí, so you should give no weight to the fact Mr O'Reilly did not go into the witness box in this case,' he said.

'In this case he did actually answer questions by the gardaí and you will have notes of those.'

He pointed out parts of the prosecution's case that he believed the jury should disregard, such as Helen Reddy's testimony about Joe telling her Rachel had definitely not been sexually assaulted.

According to the judge this could simply have been Joe just 'allaying her fears'. And he questioned Jackie Connor's evidence that Joe had told her he was afraid of being framed for Rachel's murder. 'It doesn't seem to me that that inevitably points to guilt or innocence,' he said.

Eventually, just after 3pm, the jury was sent out to decide on their verdict. Justice White told them to take as long as they needed and that if they hadn't reached a verdict by 7pm he would send them to a hotel for the night.

The 11 men and women disappeared behind the heavy brown door in the corner of the courtroom. They were now obliged to stay together and away from anyone other than the gardaí whose care they would be under until they had made their decision. All anyone could do was wait.

There were a few false alarms, but knocks on the door from the foreman turned out to be requests for markers and flip-charts or permission for the jury to go outside for a cigarette break. It all added to an increasingly tense atmosphere.

By 7pm that evening there was still no result. The jury was sent to a hotel and Joe had one more night of guaranteed freedom.

The following morning, a Saturday, there were crowds of people waiting outside the front gates of the Four Courts to gain access to the Central Criminal Court. Shortly after 10am they were opened, and within minutes Court 2 was once again crammed. It proved to be a long, sticky day with the air in the room growing unpleasantly staler by the hour.

There was no decision by lunch time, and in the afternoon various members of the Callaly family, the O'Reillys and of course the Lowes could be spotted around the courtyard, nervously smoking or chatting distractedly, anxious that this intense wait be over.

By 6pm court veterans were speculating that Justice White planned to send the jury back to the hotel for another night. It looked like the families and friends of both the victim and the accused would have to spend yet another sleepless night waiting for a verdict. The 30 or so journalists present were beginning to resign themselves to the idea that it might be Monday's papers or even possibly Tuesday's that would be reporting the verdict.

In the end there was a knock at 6.40pm, but the din of conversation in the courtroom meant that only the court clerk heard it. Quickly she crossed to the heavy brown door and disappeared for just a minute or two.

Walking back into the room she briefly looked down at the large table where the two legal teams were waiting and with a slight nod of her head she let them know there was a verdict.

Within minutes the courtroom was crammed. The Callalys did their best to remain calm as they took the seats they had occupied for the last month. Friends and supporters stood behind them, giving the odd squeeze to their arms or whispering a word or two into their ears to show their support and confidence that justice would be finally done.

At the back of the room Ann O'Reilly, her son Derek and her daughter Ann sat side by side and silent. They looked towards Joe, who could be seen swallowing hard a couple of times, as undoubtedly the realisation sank in that this was it—within minutes he would be told his fate.

There was a strange eerie silence in the courtroom as those gathered waited for Justice White to enter from his chambers. There was nothing more to say.

Solemn-faced and possibly unhappy at the huge volume of people squashed into his courtroom to witness one of the most eagerly awaited verdicts in years, the judge grimly indicated to his clerk that the jury should be brought in.

Taking their seats the jurors looked exhausted. Theirs had been a burden that nobody envied. It was confirmed that they had reached a decision after ten hours of deliberation.

A folded piece of paper was handed to the judge.

And as their verdict, which found Joe guilty of killing his wife Rachel, was read out, the courtroom erupted.

In incredible scenes, grown men and women cried while others shook their heads in disbelief. Paul, Anthony, Declan and Anne Callaly jumped to their feet and threw themselves into each others arms as screams of 'yes' and 'thank God' rang out around the courtroom.

For several minutes there was utter pandemonium as friends and supporters fought their way to get close to the Callalys to offer their tearful congratulations. In the midst of it all, Rose and Jimmy turned and embraced each other with every ounce of strength they had left. Still sitting, their faces were crumpled with raw emotion and intense relief.

At the top of the room, Joe sat wearing the same inscrutable expression as always, although perhaps a little more ashen-faced than usual. He had not even flinched as the verdict was read out. He appeared to be totally unaffected by the pandemonium going on around him.

His family also showed no emotion. His mother Ann refused to stand and just stared straight ahead. His brother and sister, grim-faced, stood and looked down at Joe.

It took several minutes for the courtroom to calm down. Justice White still had duties to carry out: he ordered Joe to stand.

His face was expressionless as he rose to his feet and faced the judge.

'You have been found guilty by this jury. The sentence prescribed for murder is one of imprisonment for life,' the judge told Joe. 'I am now imposing that sentence on you.'

Before dismissing the court for the last time, the judge thanked the jury and acknowledged the pressures they had been under during this case, which had such 'an emotionally charged atmosphere'. He also excused them from jury duty for the rest of their lives and told them that in all his years as a barrister and judge he had never seen a trial attract such intense media coverage.

He then allowed Rose to read out her victim impact statement.

Taking the stand, Rose read in her clear, firm voice the typewritten sheets she clutched with steady hands.

And many of those who had managed to resist the urge to be affected by the patent emotion already shown found it hard not to be affected by her heart-

felt words addressed to the court and to her daughter
Rachel.

'Almost three years ago Rachel kissed her beloved
Luke and Adam goodbye, and for the next twenty
minutes she was subjected to the most horrific, violent
and barbaric attack that no human should ever have to
go through,' she read to the hushed courtroom.

'We are haunted by the thought of what happened
to our beautiful daughter and sister that morning.
From that moment on, the lives of everyone who knew
Rachel and loved her were thrown into turmoil.

'Even though justice has been done, our grief
and distress will never diminish. Rachel was a truly
beautiful, loving, caring and capable girl who has left
so many memories, and she meant so much to us and
to so many—her aunts, uncles, cousins, niece and
nephews and many friends.

'Each one of us has been traumatised by feelings
of helplessness, shock, grief and the horrific reality is
that we can do nothing to bring her back. This is the
hardest part of our pain.

'Not only did Rachel leave without saying goodbye,
she also left her beloved sons, Luke and Adam,
confused scared and angry. We feel heartbroken as the
biggest damage will surely be left at their door as they
live their lives without the guidance and counselling
of their best friend.

'Rachel was never away from their side and her
harrowing loss has left a huge void in both the boys'
lives and in our lives.

'Every day we find it so difficult to accept the
devastation of her death. We struggle to come to terms

with the fact that she is now gone forever. There are days when we feel overwhelmed by grief. Sleepless nights, nightmares and panic attacks have become the norm for us. We often wake traumatised with fear by the images of terror, violence and brutality, and we wonder if we will ever return to some sense of normal life.

'We lost Rachel at the young age of 30 years and we are devastated knowing we will never be able to share with her the enjoyment of all the milestones she was so looking forward to in her life and the possibility of one day sharing with her the enjoyment of seeing her own grandchildren. As a parent it is devastating to lose a child, but under these circumstances it is unbearable.

'Rachel, if I could have given my life for you on that awful day I would have. You are such a big part of our life. Thank you for the short lifetime, which should have been so much longer and full of so many more happy memories. We treasure the memories of shared times with you. We miss you and love you so much, and not a day passes without you being remembered so lovingly.

'We hope you can now rest in peace, my darling. Your loving mam and dad, brothers, sister and sister-in-law, Declan and Denise, Paul and Denise, Anne and Anthony, and your two sons Luke and Adam.'

Rapturous applause filled the courtroom and Rose was helped down from the stand. On her way back to her family she stopped to hug Sergeant Patrick Marry, one of the main investigating officers in Rachel's murder case.

They said nothing, just held each other tightly. There was nothing to say—it was finally over.

Lined up against the walls were a number of prison officers and guards waiting to take Joe to the prison van that had been parked in the courtyard for the last two days.

The guilty man sat motionless, oblivious to the stares of those around him who were wondering what was going through his mind. His family made their way towards him.

There were no tears, just short, powerful hugs and nods of the head. Ann O'Reilly stood in front of her eldest son for some time, gripping both his arms and talking earnestly to him.

Outside, dozens of waiting photographers finally got their shot.

The Callaly family, their faces finally smiling, walked towards the flashing cameras, held each other's hands and raised their arms above their heads. 'Justice, thank God, Justice.'

CHAPTER 10

Uxoricide – The Killing of a Wife

IT HAD TAKEN almost three years, but Joe O'Reilly was finally behind bars.

The sense of relief at the verdict was unmistakable, but needless to say, it did not come without controversy.

There were those who believed the result, despite being decided upon by a jury, had been the wrong one.

Commentators, pundits and law experts told how they believed the evidence had been too circumstantial, that there had not been one shred of direct evidence, and declared the prosecution had not actually managed to place Joe at the scene of the murder.

On points of law, they argued, Joe should have been acquitted.

They also questioned the media coverage the investigation and subsequent trial had attracted, claiming Joe had been tried before he ever stepped into the courtroom.

Whether the disapproval was warranted or not, there was no denying the intense public interest in the entire affair.

Dr Robi Ludwig, a psychotherapist based in New York, is an expert in spousal homicide. A regular commentator on US television shows such as *Larry King Live* and *The Oprah Winfrey Show*, her book *Till Death Do Us Part: Love, Marriage and the Mind of a Killer Spouse* was published in 2006.

She believes there are a couple of reasons for the intense public curiosity in the Joe O'Reilly case.

'Most of us have romantic notions about meeting someone and falling in love and having the perfect relationship or marriage,' she explained.

'And most of us know that relationships do not always run smoothly. In fact, most of us, whether we admit it or not, sometimes have violent, even homicidal thoughts towards our spouse or intimate partner. And while the majority never act on those thoughts, others do, and we are fascinated with these crimes and want to understand how seemingly normal and, in many cases, flourishing lives could unravel in such devastating ways.'

And it is this 'seemingly normal' element, Dr Ludwig believes, that ultimately catches and grips the public's attention in cases like Joe's.

'Real people want to understand the motivations that drive real people over the edge,' she explained.

'Despite our fascination with the extravagance of celebrity lives, viewers may never be able to relate to them, but they can relate to the next-door neighbour whose seemingly stable marriage serves as a cover for violent impulses that explode in murderous assault.'

To Rose Callaly, her daughter's marriage never seemed anything but happy.

In an interview with RTE television the day after Joe was found guilty, she told how they had no inkling that he felt anything but love for their daughter.

'He was the person we trusted to love Rachel and look after her,' she explained.

'And we felt he had been doing that. We didn't know the full story.'[1]

Dr Ludwig believes we are all liable to being taken in by a spouse, who, after all, is essentially a stranger, not only to their partner, but to their partner's family.

'When loving couples find one another and unite, there is the hope that each partner will finally be cared for and valued,' she explained.

'The last thought people have is that they are marrying a hurtful stranger. But the truth is we all marry people who on some level are unknown to us, and part of what intrigues us about couples who express their violent feelings is that they are more like us than not.'

Through her extensive research into spousal murder, Dr Ludwig identified ten personality types, ranging from the Betrayal/Abandonment Killer (who loses control and kills from a broken heart) to the Black Widow/Profit Killer (who kills for money).

After discussing Joe's case, she suggested he displayed characteristics of both the Narcissistic Killer and the Sociopathic Killer.

'The sociopath knows the difference between right and wrong; he just doesn't care about it,' her book explains.

'Instead he follows his own rules and laws. Although not all sociopaths are killers, their lack of feeling and tendency to devalue human life, along with their inclination to feel victimised and rejected, makes them much more inclined to consider murder as an option.'

She explained how many sociopaths appear to the outside world.

'They can come across as self-assured, dominating and arrogant,' she believes. 'But he can also be glib, charming and ingratiating.'

Many of those who investigated and followed the trial were particularly struck by just how cold and callous Joe had been about organising and carrying out his wife's killing.

First of all he made sure it was Rachel's mother who found her brutalised body, an image that will undoubtedly haunt her for the rest of her life.

And when he arrived at his son's school to collect him on the day of the murder, the principal remembers seeing Joe from a window, standing by the side of sports pitch, as though waiting for something.

He was waiting. Not everything in his plan was in place at the time; Rose still had to arrive at the scene.

And when he arrived back to Naul, he began to walk into the house with his youngest son, Adam, in tow. Only that a neighbour insisted that the young boy stay with her, Adam would probably have seen the body of his battered mother.

'What makes sociopaths so dangerous is their amazing ability to rationalise outrageous behaviour and dismiss personal responsibility for their actions,' says Dr Ludwig. 'They give little thought to the pain and degradation they impose on their victims, in part because they don't really care. They will do whatever it takes to satisfy their needs.

'They don't kill because they are necessarily distressed or for the more "logical" precipitating factors such as jealousy or rage. Instead they kill in a straightforward and uncomplicated way. Sometimes they even see themselves as the true victims and are able to rationalise their behaviour, which helps them to dismiss personal responsibility for their actions.

'Sociopaths typically are calm and collected. It's not hard for them to appear like everything is under control.'

Dr Ludwig also mentioned the possibility of Joe having elements of the Narcissistic Killer in his character.

'The person who suffers from a narcissistic personality disorder does not really love himself but only seems to,' she says.

'What he really loves is the reflection of himself or the image he projects. They crave admiration and are junkies for positive feedback from others. When they do not get the desired reaction, it becomes virtually impossible for them to feel whole or complete.'

Dr Ludwig said the natural and normal change in Joe and Rachel's marriage after their sons were born could have triggered his plan to murder Rachel and then marry Nikki Pelley.

'Having kids may have been the straw that broke the camel's back,' she said.

'Many husbands feel they are no longer the centre of attention, no longer the focus; he was not getting the same attention that he used to when there was just him and his wife.'

This situation, she suggested, could have led to feelings of extreme anger and prompted him to change things, whatever it took and whatever the possible consequences.

'It could be that he was so intensely angry and blaming his wife, so the solution is to get rid of the bad wife and slip the new one right in there,' she explained.

'Criminal minds are all so different, but there are those who push the limit to the point where they don't understand how their actions are going to have long-term effects.

'So they are not thinking, "If I kill my wife, maybe it's not going to work out all perfectly, maybe they'll find out that I killed my wife." They're just thinking about feeling good. It's a very self-referential, egocentric way of operating in that way and that's what usually trips them up.'

It is clear that however clever Joe thought he was during his careful planning, he was distracted by his intense feelings towards his wife and also probably by his feelings towards his lover.

'A person who falls "in hate" may spend as much time thinking and brooding about the hated individual as does a person who falls in love,' Dr Ludwig explains.

'Accompanying hatred, however, is a tremendous amount of aggression and hostility. Hate can blind us and therefore make us think and behave in ways beyond reason. Hate is the most powerful and enduring form of primal hostility.

'The bottom line is that anyone can become a spousal killer or a victim. In most cases nothing will ever happen, but the potential is there, and I think that is what contributes to the interest in cases like this. It's the curiosity of a relationship gone so badly wrong. It's within our DNA to be homicidal when we have to, and very often when it comes down to committing the crime, in that moment of time they [killers] feel they have to do something like this in order to survive.

'Murder fascinates us, in part because the desire to kill another comes from the deepest part of us, our unconscious. Even for the sociopath, they feel the spouse is interfering with their ultimate happiness and they are disposable. It's very much, "Is it going to be you or me?" And they choose themselves.

'What is very interesting about marital homicide is that very often these people are not career criminals,' she added. 'Something happens within the marital relationship that they feel is directed primarily towards them and so they react. And you know, in general, spousal killers come from very normal backgrounds, with normal families; that's what makes them so scary.'

Given Joe's apparent 'normality', perhaps it is not surprising that his family still insist he is innocent.

'My son is not a murderer. If I had thought that for one minute I wouldn't have had him in my house,' his mother, Ann O'Reilly, said after the verdict. [2]

'He is my son and I know he is not capable of doing what they said he did. I know he is not the only innocent person locked up in jail,' she added.

'I have first-hand experience of how this can happen because of my own brother Christy spent years locked up after being accused of a murder he did not do.

'Christy is the most inoffensive man you could ever meet . . . It took Christy years to clear his name, and I know in the end that Joe will as well and the full truth will come out.'

Her other son, Derek, was equally adamant that the family would not rest until Joe's innocence was proved.

'We are seeking legal advice to see what steps we can take as quickly as possible to address this miscarriage of justice. We love Joe and we will never stop supporting him.' [3]

Rose, on the other hand, a woman who had known and loved Joe for more than a decade, said she had suspected him from the beginning.

'That day [of the murder] when Joe came into the house his first words were, "Jesus, Rachel, what did you do?"' she later told RTE News. [4]

'I remember thinking to myself, "What does he mean? Rachel was murdered. What could she have done?" Joe didn't lift Rachel into his arms—he certainly didn't utter any words of love, which I found odd.

'Jim said to me that's probably shock. People react differently. But I would have expected some form of emotion even if Joe didn't love Rachel at that stage. Even if he didn't love her, she was the mother of his two children.'

It took her husband Jim a little longer to come to the same conclusion.

'I was probably pushing it around my mind and one day Rose said to me, "You're going to have to take it on board, Jim; it was him,"' he explained.

'The police came down one day and said to us: "There is no one else out there who did this. We have taken in every suspect all around the area and there is no one else."' [5]

It had been a hard-earned victory for the gardaí. And although Joe was ultimately found guilty, they knew it had been a close call. If Joe had left his mobile phone in the office that morning, he would have almost definitely gotten away with murder.

It helped once again prove the invaluable role that mobile phone technology can now play in investigations of this type. In August 2002, the public watched in grim fascination as the net slowly closed around Ian Huntley in one of Britain's most famous murder cases.

Huntley abducted and killed Holly Wells and Jessica Chapman, two ten-year-old girls from Soham.

He was eventually charged and brought to justice only because detectives were able to prove that Jessica's phone was switched off inside or outside his house.

It was not the first time that the investigation team in the Rachel O'Reilly case had been reminded of Huntley.

Joe's willingness to keep in regular contact with several journalists in the aftermath of Rachel's murder led a number of officers to describe his actions as 'Huntley-esque'—a reference to the television appearances and media interviews the Soham killer did before his arrest for the murders of Holly and Jessica.

Of course, mobile phone evidence had been used in Ireland before.

'This [Joe's guilty verdict] wasn't the first major conviction secured with such technical evidence,' explained Felix McKenna, former commander of the Criminal Assets Bureau. [6]

'Brian Meehan was convicted of the murder of journalist Veronica Guerin on foot of phone traffic between his handset and that of associate of Russell Warren. It should come as no surprise that he [Joe] was convicted on a body of mainly circumstantial evidence.

'Over my career I can recall cases where someone was convicted on circumstantial evidence while the accused often walked free in other cases where there was direct evidence. Crucial for the jury [in Joe's case] was the fact that much of this evidence came from independent third parties, reputable members of the public with no axe to grind.

'Obviously the phone evidence, which destroyed O'Reilly's alibi, was central.'

Chief Superintendent Mick Finnegan, who headed the investigation, agreed: 'Never before have we placed such reliance on mobile-phone and other technologies. It has become vital in the fight against crime simply because criminals have become so much more sophisticated.' [7]

✤ ✤ ✤ ✤ ✤

Officially known as prisoner 42807, Joe spent his first night behind bars at the Mountjoy Prison complex. He slept that evening in a padded cell, standard procedure for any criminal sentenced to life, in case they might try to kill themselves.

The following day he was transferred to the Midlands Prison in Portlaoise where he is expected to serve at least 12 years.

Since his incarceration dozens of stories about his new life have appeared in the media, ranging from whether or not he is attending the gym to his new-found faith. His interest in the Jehovah's Witness movement was confirmed in a newspaper interview by an Irish spokesman for the group, Mark O'Malley, a week after Joe was imprisoned.

'Joe has studied the Bible with different Jehovah's Witnesses and he has attended several meetings,' he said. [8]

'We will study with different individuals on and off. Sometimes people will come to our meetings regularly and then we might not see them for a while. Joe would fit into that category.'

It was also reported that before his trial he had started the process to claim Rachel's life insurance policy, worth €194,000. And he submitted her death certificate in order to have the mortgage on their home settled.

If Joe had been acquitted, he stood to make a total of €434,000 on the two policies. The insurance companies had refused to pay out until a verdict was reached in his trial.

As for his former mistress, Nikki, she visited him in jail a week to the day after he was convicted. Looking tired and drawn, she spent an hour talking to him at the prison. It's believed she still regularly makes the trip to the Midlands prison. Most recently it was reported by one Sunday newspaper that the pair still plan to marry.

✤ ✤ ✤ ✤ ✤

The two victims affected most by this tragedy are probably still too young to fully understand what has been going on around them.

All that Luke and Adam O'Reilly can be certain of is that first they lost their mother, and now their father has disappeared too. The long-term effects on the boys are unimaginable.

For a man who professed to be a 'good father' and to love his children greatly, it is hard to understand how he could have allowed them to experience such a devastating loss, not once but twice.

'All of our family feel the boys were the victims,' said Rose later.

'She was just ripped from them. She kissed them goodbye going to school and held their hand that morning and that breaks our heart.

'The person who murdered her knew, as she picked them up and left them into school, that their loving mother was never going to see them again and, as Marie Cassidy said, she had nothing in her stomach even.

'That would have been Rachel, she wouldn't have thought of a breakfast until she'd come home. She would look after them first. That was the last memory of her.' [9]

ENDNOTES

CHAPTER ONE

1. Ken Foy, the *Irish Daily Star on Sunday*, 22 July 2007. 'I will be the first to visit Joe in prison.'
2. Kathy Sheridan, *The Irish Times*, 23 July 2007. 'O'Reilly made a calculated effort to sow suspicion among Rachel's friends.'
3. Kathy Sheridan, *The Irish Times*, 23 July 2007. 'O'Reilly made a calculated effort to sow suspicion among Rachel's friends.'
4. Mark Hilliard and Eoin Reynolds, the *Irish Daily Star on Sunday*, 22 July 2007.
5. Kathy Sheridan, *The Irish Times*, 23 July 2007. 'O'Reilly made a calculated effort to sow suspicion among Rachel's friends.'
6. Kathy Sheridan, *The Irish Times*, 23 July 2007. 'O'Reilly made a calculated effort to sow suspicion among Rachel's friends.'
7. Breda Heffernan and Dearbhail McDonald, *The Irish Independent*, 23 July 2007. 'Rachel "in love" with killer Joe up to the brutal end.'
8. Evidence given at Joe O'Reilly's trial.

CHAPTER TWO

1. Evidence given at Joe O'Reilly's trial.
2. Evidence given at Joe O'Reilly's trial.
3. Evidence given at Joe O'Reilly's trial.
4. Evidence given at Joe O'Reilly's trial.
5. Evidence given at Joe O'Reilly's trial.
6. Kathy Sheridan, *The Irish Times*, 23 July 2007. 'O'Reilly made

a calculated effort to sow suspicion among Rachel's friends.'

7. Kathy Sheridan, *The Irish Times*, 23 July 2007. 'O'Reilly made a calculated effort to sow suspicion among Rachel's friends.'

8. Evidence given at Joe O'Reilly's trial.

9. Evidence given at Joe O'Reilly's trial.

CHAPTER THREE

1. Evidence given at Joe O'Reilly's trial.

2. Interview with Orla O'Donnell for *RTE television news*, 22 July 2007.

3. Evidence given at Joe O'Reilly's trial.

4. Evidence given at Joe O'Reilly's trial.

5. Caoimhe Young and Nicola Tallant, *The Sunday World*, 22 July 2007. 'Mum Rose tells court: "Rachel, if I could have given my life for yours that day I would have."'

CHAPTER FIVE

1. Joanne McElgunn, *The Irish Mirror*, 28 October 2004. 'Rachel's Hubby Denies Affair.'

2. Interview with author.

3. Lisa O'Connor, *The Irish Sunday Mirror*, 21 November 2004. 'Murder Case Mum; My Son's no Killer.'

4. Dearbhail McDonald, *The Sunday Times*, 13 March 2005. 'Coffin letter May Reveal Identity of Rachel's Killer.'

CHAPTER TEN

1. Interview with Orla O'Donnell, *RTE television news*, 22 July 2007.

2. Nicola Byrne, the *Irish Mail on Sunday*, 22 July 2007. 'He's my son, I love him and I know he's innocent.'

3. Nicola Byrne, the *Irish Mail on Sunday*, 22 July 2007. 'He's my son, I love him and I know he's innocent.'

4. Interview with Orla O'Donnell, *RTE television news*, 22 July 2007.

5. Interview with Orla O'Donnell, *RTE television news*, 22 July 2007.

6. Felix McKenna, the *Evening Herald*, 23 July 2007. 'O'Reilly verdict does justice to the Irish law system.'

7. Shane Phelan, the *Irish Daily Mail*, 23 July 2007. 'Technology spoilt "Perfect Murder".'

8. Caitriona Gaffney and Niall Donald, the *Irish Daily Star on Sunday*, 29 July 2007.

9. Interview with Orla O'Donnell, *RTE television news*, 22 July 2007.

MORE NON-FICTION FROM MAVERICK HOUSE

CONFESSIONS

THE INTIMATE ADVENTURES OF A LAP DANCER

By BILLIEGEAN
WITH YVONNE KINSELLA

Confessions is the story of a young woman making her way in the world. That way just happens to be in the sex industry. Billiegean gives a no-holds-barred expose of what goes on behind the velvet curtains of the lap dancing clubs.

Caught up in a party scene where drugs and alcohol were a daily occurrence, she lived a hedonistic life, forsaking all others, including her little girl.

From glamour modelling to wet t-shirt competitions, mud wrestling to sex chat-lines, lap dancing to stripping, Billie's done it all.

With her honest yet humorous take on the sex industry that she knows so well, *Confessions* is a book you won't be able to put down.

To order this book go to www.maverickhouse.com

MORE NON FICTION BY MAVERICK HOUSE

BLOOD AND MONEY

By DAVE COPELAND

Filled with paranoid mobsters, clever scams, and deep betrayals, *Blood and Money* gives a unique insight into one of the most successful gangs ever to operate on American soil.

By the time Ron Gonen arrived in New York City he had broken out of prison in Germany, been exiled from Israel, fled England as a prime suspect in a multi-million dollar crime ring, and had been chased out of Guatemala. Gonen lived life in the fast lane until things spiralled out of control.

In the 1980s, a small group of Israeli nationals set up one of the most lucrative crime syndicates in New York City's history. With rackets ranging from drug dealing to contract killings, their crime spree was so violent that it wasn't long before they were dubbed the 'Israeli Mafia'.

The gang went to war with the Italian mafia, killed Russian gangsters and pulled off the biggest gold heist in the history of Manhattan's Diamond District.

They would have become the most powerful gang in the New York underworld had Gonen not decided to risk his life and become an FBI informant. *Blood and Money* is his story.

'A thrilling guts-and-glory look inside the Israeli organised crime machine of 1980s New York City.' - Publishers Weekly

To order this book go to www.maverickhouse.com

MORE NON-FICTION FROM MAVERICK HOUSE

THE LAST EXECUTIONER

Memoirs of thailand's last Prison Executioner

By CHAVORET JARUBOON
with NICOLA PIERCE

Chavoret Jaruboon was personally responsible for executing 55 prison inmates on Thailand's infamous death row.

As a boy, he wanted to be a teacher like his father, then a rock'n'roll star like Elvis, but his life changed when he joined Thailand's prison service. From there he took on one of the hardest jobs in the world.

Honest and often disturbing—but told with surprising humour and emotion—*The Last Executioner* is the remarkable story of one man's experiences with life and death.

Emotional and at times confronting, the book grapples with the controversial topic of the death sentence and makes no easy reading.

This book is not for the faint-hearted—*The Last Executioner* takes you right behind the bars of the Bangkok Hilton and into death row.

'Not afraid to tell it like it is.' - IPS Asia

'A truly remarkable story.' - Manchester Weekly News

'Grisly, yet riveting reading.' - The Big Chilli, Thailand.

To order this book go to www.maverickhouse.com

MORE NON-FICTION FROM MAVERICK HOUSE

LOOT

INSIDE THE WORLD OF STOLEN ART

BY THOMAS MCSHANE
WITH DARY MATERA

Thomas McShane is one of the world's foremost authorities on the art theft business. With great energy and imagination, *Loot* recounts some of his most thrilling cases as he matches wits with Mafia mobsters and smooth criminals.

Covering his 36 years as an FBI Agent, the author brings us on a thrilling ride through the underworld of stolen art and historical artefacts as he dons his many disguises and aliases to chase down $900 million worth of stolen art pieces.

McShane has worked on high profile cases all over the world, including the Beit heist in Ireland. From Rembrandts robbed in Paris to van Goghs vanishing in New York, McShane's tale is one of great adventure, told with surprising humour.

The Thomas Crown Affair meets *Donnie Brasco* in this story of a truly extraordinary life.

To order this book go to www.maverickhouse.com

MORE NON-FICTION FROM MAVERICK HOUSE

TILL DEATH DO US PART

THE TRUE STORY OF MISGUIDED LOVE, MARRIAGE, DEATH AND DECEPTION

BY SIOBHÁN GAFFNEY

Young, handsome Colin Whelan was a magnet for women, who always fell for his seductive charms. Little did they know that underneath his cool exterior lay a twisted desire to kill.

Behind the facade of normality lay a psychopathic mind struggling to control its homicidal urges. Having seduced and married his sweetheart Mary Gough, Whelan immediately began planning her brutal murder.

While his young wife dreamed of a love-filled marriage, Whelan searched the internet for information on serial killers and the methods they used to strangle their victims.

Compelling and disturbing, this book reveals how Whelan murdered his wife to claim a hefty life insurance policy and how he faked his own suicide when he became the prime suspect for the murder.

Till Death Do Us Part offers a fascinating insight into the true motivation behind one of Ireland's most notorious murders. It is a horrifying story of love, lust, revenge and murder - all the more shocking because every word is true.

To order this book go to www.maverickhouse.com

MORE NON FICTION BY MAVERICK HOUSE

NOT ON OUR WATCH

By DON CHEADLE
AND JOHN PRENDERGAST

If you care about issues of genocide and other mass atrocities, but you just don't know what to do and you truly want to make a difference, this book was written for you.

Mass murder. Rape. Torture. Starvation. The brutality of civil war in places like Sudan, Northern Uganda, Congo, and Somalia seems far away and impossible to solve. Six million graves have been freshly dug during the last couple of decades in this modern-day holocaust, and many millions of people have been driven from their homes.

Angered by the devastating violence that has engulfed Darfur and other war zones in Africa, famed actor Don Cheadle teamed up with leading human-rights activist John Prendergast to shine a haunting spotlight on these atrocities. Here, they candidly reveal heart-wrenching personal accounts of their experiences visiting Darfur and Northern Uganda, and highlight the stories of extraordinary people who are taking a stand against genocide and other mass atrocities.

The book outlines six inspiring strategies that every one of us can adopt to help bring about change. No personal action is too small. For the sanctity of the human race, it is imperative that we not stand idly by as innocent civilians.

Take a stand. Raise your voice. Find out how *you* can make a difference. The time to act is now.

'A compelling account of the gravest humanitarian crisis of our time.' - Martin Bell, UNICEF Ambassador.

MORE NON-FICTION FROM MAVERICK HOUSE

WELCOME TO HELL

ONE MAN'S FIGHT FOR LIFE INSIDE THE 'BANGKOK HILTON'

BY COLIN MARTIN

Written from his cell and smuggled out page by page, Colin Martin's autobiography chronicles an innocent man's struggle to survive inside one of the world's most dangerous prisons.

After being swindled out of a fortune, Martin was let down by the hopelessly corrupt Thai police. Forced to rely upon his own resources, he tracked down the man who conned him and, drawn into a fight, accidentally stabbed and killed the man's bodyguard.

Martin was arrested, denied a fair trial, convicted of murder and thrown into prison—where he remained for eight years. Honest and often disturbing, *Welcome to Hell* is the remarkable story of how Martin was denied justice again and again.

In his extraordinary account, he describes the swindle, his arrest and vicious torture by police, the unfair trial, and the eight years of brutality and squalor he was forced to endure.

To order this book go to www.maverickhouse.com

MORE NON FICTION BY MAVERICK HOUSE

HEROIN

A True Story of Drug Addiction, Hope and Triumph

By JULIE O'TOOLE

Heroin is a story of hope, a story of a young woman's emergence from the depths of drug addiction and despair.

Julie O'Toole started using heroin in her mid-teens. A bright young girl, she quickly developed a chronic addiction, and her life spiralled out of control. Enslaved to the drug, Julie began shoplifting to feed her habit before offering to work as a drug dealer for notorious gangsters. She was eventually saved by the care and support of a drugs counsellor and by her own strength to endure.

Her story takes us from Dublin's inner city to London and America. With honesty and insight, Julie tells of the horror and degradation that came with life as a drug addict, and reveals the extraordinary strength of will that enabled her to conquer heroin addiction and to help others do the same.

To order this book go to www.maverickhouse.com

MORE NON FICTION BY MAVERICK HOUSE

NIGHTMARE IN LAOS

By KAY DANES

Hours after her husband Kerry was kidnapped by the Communist Laos government, Kay Danes tried to flee to Thailand with her two youngest children, only to be intercepted at the border.

Torn away from them and sent to an undisclosed location, it was then that the nightmare really began. Forced to endure 10 months of outrageous injustice and corruption, she and her husband fought for their freedom from behind the filth and squalor of one of Laos' secret gulags.

Battling against a corrupt regime, she came to realise that there were many people worse off held captive in Laos—people without a voice, or any hope of freedom. Kay had to draw from the strength and spirit of those around her in order to survive this hidden hell, while the world media and Australian government tried desperately to have her and Kerry freed before it was too late and all hope was lost.

For Kay, the sorrow and pain she saw people suffer at the hands of the regime in Laos, where human rights are non-existent, will stay with her forever, and she vowed to tell the world what she has seen. This is her remarkable story.

To order this book go to www.maverickhouse.com

MORE NON FICTION BY MAVERICK HOUSE

THE MIRACLE OF FATIMA MANSIONS

AN ESCAPE FROM DRUG ADDICTION

By SHAY BYRNE

The Miracle of Fatima Mansions is the moving story of a teenage boy who lost himself to drug addiction after the death of his father.

Set against the backdrop of working-class Dublin in the 1970s, Shay Byrne has written a brutally honest account of his addiction, his crimes and his redemption.

Byrne narrowly escaped death during a violent attack at Fatima Mansions, the flat complex synonymous with extreme social depravation, social decay and drugs. It was the unlikely location of an epiphany that would transform his life.

The incident forced Byrne to confront his inner demons and seek help at a radical treatment centre.

Told with searing honesty, Byrne's debut book is the most insightful, candid and thought-provoking book ever written on Dublin's drug culture. It is destined to become a classic.

To order this book go to www.maverickhouse.com